Thinking Things Through

Problem Solving in Mathematics

Leone Burton

Basil Blackwell

© Leone Burton 1984
First published 1984

Published by
Basil Blackwell Limited
108 Cowley Road
Oxford OX4 1JF

British Library Cataloguing in Publication Data

Burton, Leone
Thinking things through.
1. Mathematics—Study and teaching
(Elementary)
I. Title
372.7'3   QA135.5

ISBN 0–631–13813–7

Typeset by Oxford Publishing Services in 11/13 pt. Palatino
Printed in Great Britain by Dotesios (Printers) Ltd. Bradford-on-Avon, Wiltshire

510
BUR

α

Thinking Things Through

Problem Solving in Mathematics

136223

To Mark, who spends his time creating problems (often for me) and resolving them (usually without my help) and whose energy for problem solving seems inexhaustible, with my love.

CONTENTS

ACKNOWLEDGEMENTS

I am indebted to the editor of *Mathematics Teaching* for permission to use material from my article 'What can you find out about odd and even numbers?' in Chapter 1; and to Francis Lowenthal, University of Mons, Belgium, for details of the geoboard work in Chapter 2. The problem pack was originally compiled in collaboration with Janet Duffin, Claire Hill, Sister Mary Timothy Pinner and Kaye Stacey.

L. Burton

INTRODUCTION

Many teachers in both primary and secondary schools are interested in starting problem solving in their mathematics classrooms. This book is a manual to encourage this to happen. It developed from a research project supported by the Social Science Research Council, directed by the author and run in collaboration with more than 30 teachers and 850 pupils aged between nine and 13 years.

Recently, advocates of real problem solving have urged the use of problems from the real world in classrooms. This can be a most fruitful approach to the applications of mathematics. However, the author believes that problem solving is only real when pupils take responsibility for their own mathematical thinking. Whereas many teachers find the difficulties of introducing real-world problems somewhat daunting, the approach advocated here has the advantage of being simpler to administer and open to small beginnings.

The teachers who worked on the study were asked to spend only one hour per week using the problem-solving materials. But during that hour they were asked to change their role from one of responsibility for what the pupils do and learn to one of resource for the pupils. They were encouraged not to provide answers or methods but to provoke their pupils into searching for these themselves. The notion of responsibility was a key one – pupils taking responsibility for their choice of problem, their working partners and method of attack, their thinking and their results. This produces a profound change in classroom relationships and climate. Teachers were impressed by what their pupils could and would do and by how this understanding was demonstrated.

A change like this can be threatening even though its effects are rewarding; it is the intention of this book to support teachers who are interested in developing this kind of work. Since the project concluded, many in-service sessions have been run with teachers demonstrating the how and why of the approach. A number of relevant and practical questions are usually asked:

What is so different about problem solving?
Why is it important to the pupils' mathematical experience?
Where do I find problems which are suitable?
How do I introduce the problems in class?
What do I do about the range of ability?
How do I tell that the pupils have benefited?
How do I tell what the pupils have benefited?

Each of these questions is answered in a chapter of this book. The purpose is to provide a range of problems together with a rationale for

1

how and why these problems might affect the approach of pupils and teachers. Pupils accepted all the problems as challenges and were subsequently highly motivated. The problems do not teach: they offer the teacher an opportunity to observe the quality and ingenuity of pupils' mathematical thinking. For the pupils they offer time to use the mathematical skills, knowledge and above all the processes, with which they feel comfortable, doing challenging tasks which are open to their own interpretation.

Once the approach is established there is no shortage of problems; however, further resources are listed in the Bibliography. Once teachers become accustomed to hearing the pupils' questions these can be adopted as new problems. In addition, once a method is perceived for turning exercises back into the problems they originally reflected, extensive resources are available in existing texts. Chapter 1 begins with an example of how to do this, with pupils' work demonstrating the results of the different approaches.

In the development of this work the author was extremely lucky to have the support and help of colleagues who later became good friends. In particular, Janet Duffin, Claire Hill and Sandy Mahon have contributed to the thinking in this volume. But most of all credit is due to the pupils, and their teachers who unstintingly gave of their time and their thoughts so that these ideas could be tried and evaluated. To them, a most grateful thank-you.

1 WHAT MAKES PROBLEM SOLVING DIFFERENT?

This question was given to some 12-year-old pupils:

O stands for any odd number.
E stands for any even number.
Write down what you get in the following addition sums.

O + O =
E + E =
E + O =
O + O + O =
O + O + O + O =
O + O + E + O =
O + O + O + O + O =

Describe in words what you will get if you add together *any* number of odd numbers.

Figure 1 shows what Richard wrote:

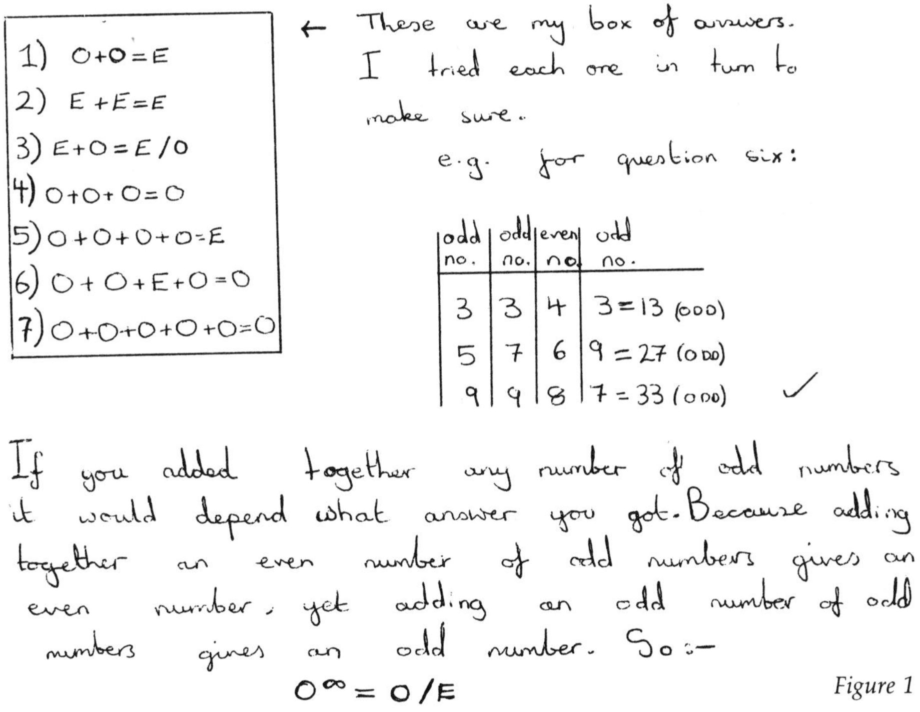

← These are my box of answers.
I tried each one in turn to
make sure.
        e.g. for question six:

1) O+O = E
2) E + E = E
3) E+O = E / O
4) O+O+ O= O
5) O+O+O+O = E
6) O + O+E+O = O
7) O+O+O+O +O= O

odd no.	odd no.	even no.	odd no.
3	3	4	3 = 13 (ood)
5	7	6	9 = 27 (ooo)
9	9	8	7 = 33 (ooo) ✓

If you added together any number of odd numbers
it would depend what answer you got. Because adding
together an even number of odd numbers gives an
even number, yet adding an odd number of odd
numbers gives an odd number. So :—
$$O^\infty = O / E$$

Figure 1

3

> If I used this method, I would almost certainly have a sign for using in an answer where the answer could be even or odd. e.g.= So:—
>
> $$O^{\infty} = \text{Ⓞ/E}$$

The rules in this are as follows :

O+O	ALWAYS	equals	E
E+O	ALWAYS	equals	E
O^{∞}	ALWAYS	equals	Ⓞ/E
O+E	ALWAYS	equals	Ⓞ/E

Another 12-year-old pupil was asked: 'What happens when you add together odd and even numbers?' This is what happened. First he wrote:

$$5 + 6 = 11 \qquad O + E = O$$
$$E + O = O$$
$$10 + 9 = 19 \qquad E + O = O$$
$$E + O = O$$

Pupil: *Do you mind my using Os and Es?*
Teacher: *It's your problem. You use what you like!*

He then wrote:

firmly ringing the statement and added:

$$\text{always} \quad \text{because}$$
$$O = E - 1 \quad \text{So} \quad E + E - 1 = E - 1$$

Pupil: *That's my first theorem.*

Figure 2 shows the way he continued:

4

Figure 2

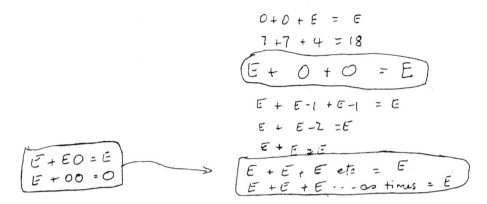

Suddenly he decided that an example was needed so he wrote:

$$E + E - 1 + E - 1 + E - 1 = \sharp 0$$

followed by:

$$E + E - 3 = 0$$

Teacher: *Oh, I see. You have already said that $E + E = E$, so that is why $E + E - 3$ is odd, because it must be the same as $E - 1$, which you said was odd.*

Pupil: *No, that's all wrong. I must have made a mistake. You can't do that.*

Teacher: *But I am only taking what you have written down already. You said that any number of Es are always E when added together. So $E + E$ is E and -3 is the same as $E - 1$, or $E + 1$, which you have already said is 0.*

Pupil: *No, no, no! That's all right when you are talking about any even or odd number. But $E - 3$ is a particular number and you can't go playing tricks with it like that. I must have done something wrong. I know, I'll put numbers in and see what happens.*

He went back to his previous statement and added the superscripts you see below. He wrote:

$$\overset{}{E} + \overset{3}{E} - 1 + \overset{1}{E} - 1 + \overset{3}{E} - 1 = \sharp 0$$
$$E + E - 3 = 0$$
$$E + E - E - 1 = 0$$

Teacher: *Imagine that I have asked four people to think of an even number. I will represent their thoughts like this:*

Now each person is asked to take one from their number:

Does that help with your problem?

Pupil: All right – if you will allow this:

$$E = E - E - 1 = E - E - 1 = 0$$

then I will allow this:

$$E - E - 1 = E - 1 = 0'.$$

He wrote:

$$E - E - 1 = 0$$
$$E - 1 = 0$$

Figure 3 illustrates how he continued with his problem:

$$0 + 0 = E$$
$$1 + 1 = 2$$
$$3 + 3 = 6$$

$$0 + 0 = E$$

$$0 + 0 + 0 = 0$$
$$1 + 1 + 1 = 3$$
$$3 + 3 + 3 = 9$$

$$0 + 0 + 0 + 0 = E$$
$$1 + 1 + 1 + 1 = 4$$

$$0 + 0 + 0 = 0$$

$$0 0 = 0$$
$$E 0 = E$$

$$0 + 0 + 0 = 0$$
$$0 + 0 = E$$
$$0 \times 3 = 0$$
$$0 \times 2 = E$$
$$E - 1 + E - 1 + E - 1 = 0$$
$$E - 3 = 0$$
$$E + E(-1) = 0$$

Figure 3

Then suddenly he wrote:

$$\times \; = \; +$$
$$- \; = \; \div$$

and got up and walked away.

Teacher: *Hold on. You can't just get up and walk away without explaining to me what is going on here* (pointing to the final two statements).

Pupil: *Oh, I've finished that problem. If I've done it for +, I've done it for ×, and if I've done it for −, I've done it for ÷.*

Teacher: *Are you really telling me that you know that your statements for + are always true for ×, and your statements for − and ÷ would be true in the same way? How do you know that? Is it really true?*

Pupil: *I don't care . . . if you like. . .*

What similarities are there between the work of the first and second pupil? Both depended upon specialising, clothing the abstract notation in actual numbers. But whereas both started out trying special cases in order to construct a statement, such as $O + E = O$, the second pupil went on to make conjectures and used his specialising to test these. Hence, for example, he stated that $O + O = E$, then checked with $1 + 1$ and $3 + 3$. The pupils invented a notation, the first pupil using $O_\infty = O/E$ which would, presumably, read 'the sum of any number of odd numbers can give either an odd or an even answer'. However, the second pupil began by introducing the very notation which had been given in the statement of the problem. He went on to investigate the combinations which had been offered in the statement of the problem but then took his investigation further, moving into multiplication and arriving at a formal expression of the generalisation which the first pupil had been asked to provide in words: $OO = O$, $EO = E$.

It is interesting that both pupils ran into difficulties with $E + O$. The first pupil simply states that $E + O$ can equal O or E. He does not appear to have tested this assertion so signs of the thinking that lay behind it are unavailable. The second pupil encountered a difficulty when the particularity of -3 caused the generality of $E-3$ to wobble. Only after spending time building up cases again, was his generalisation reinstated. Whereas the problem for the first pupil was prescribed by the demands in the question, for the second pupil, the problem was an exploration which came to a climax with his articulation of the relationships $\times = +$, $- = \div$. Not only was he satisfied that he had arrived at a conclusion, but what was particularly pleasing was that his conclusion offered another problem: is his final assertion justified?

The result of both pupils' work might well have been the same. We have no way of knowing what they took away from doing this particular piece of work. It is clear, however, that when you work with children in the classroom their attitudes to the work will be very different. In the first case, the pupil is responding in a fairly classic way to the kind of demand made in a mathematics lesson. The work is neatly presented; the results clearly displayed. The pupil has met the requirements.

In the second case the pupil felt that he was creating something and, indeed, he did. Much emotional energy was expended in the process and, consequently, a deeper commitment was made to the conclusions. Furthermore, his creativity has made possible some future action either by himself, or by another pupil. One pupil described the two different procedures in poignant terms: 'You start out looking through a small opening. With the first presentation, it is as if the furthest you can see is a wall. With the second presentation, you can go on looking further and further into the distance.'

When the first presentation was shown to the pupil who had done the second piece of work, he said with some dismay, 'Oh. It's all there!' When asked whether he would have preferred to be given the question in that form, he said: 'No, absolutely not. I don't like doing other people's questions. It is much more interesting to make the question your own'.

2 WHY IS PROBLEM SOLVING IMPORTANT?

In 1982 the Cockcroft Report stated: 'The ability to solve problems is at the heart of mathematics'. It continued, 'The idea of investigation is fundamental both to the study of mathematics itself and also to an understanding of the ways in which mathematics can be used to extend knowledge and to solve problems in very many fields' (paragraph 250); and went further: 'Mathematical exploration and investigations are of value even when they are not directed specifically to the learning of new concepts' (paragraph 322).

Does this view of mathematics accord with the experience of most pupils in our primary and secondary schools? Unfortunately not. For them, mathematics consists of a collection of facts together with some skills. The facts must be remembered; the skills practised. Along the way, belief in common sense is often suspended and mathematical mystery embraced. Hence the patently absurd answers often offered by pupils to questions posed by their teachers. For example, a 13-year-old pupil asked to write down the result of subtracting 70 from 109 offered the answer 100 and yet when the question was couched in terms of money he used the counting-on algorithm most efficiently to find the answer *mentally*. This pupil helped in his parents' shop on a Saturday and was most adept at mental arithmetic. Yet at school, he was in the remedial class and as the above demonstrates, his ability to apply taught procedures was faulty in the extreme. As a problem solver, he was probably not bad at all and certainly he had acquired personal procedures which he could rely on. What was lacking for him, as for so many pupils, was a clear demonstration of the relationship between what he already had in terms of skills and procedures, and what was being used and taught in the mathematics classroom. Too often, pupils lack confidence and competency. We observe a negative attitude to mathematics and an expectation by pupils of failure.

All three quotations from the Report focus on active investigation and exploration. Mathematics is certainly a *doing* subject, whether at the service of another discipline or in its own right. Mathematics is used to solve useful problems; it can be played with in a creative way to see what can be discovered; it is the basis on which amusing and intriguing puzzles can be invented; it has great power to inform. All these are surely good reasons for a problem-solving approach to the doing of mathematics. But they are not the best reason. The greatest value of this approach is in the effect it has on the classroom. Hesitancy and dependency in pupils are replaced by confidence and autonomy. Dislike of mathematics turns to enjoyment, indeed enthusiasm. Low self-images are replaced by expressions of authority. The change in pedagogical style gives teachers the opportunity, sometimes for the first time, to observe pupils and listen to their discussions. They frequently express amazement at what their pupils do and do not understand, can and cannot do. This is not to suggest that problem solving is a universal panacea for all the difficulties of mathematics learning and teaching. But in those classrooms where even limited amounts of problem solving have been tried, teachers and pupils comment favourably on its effects.

The overwhelming importance of problem solving, therefore, is in the opportunity it provides for teachers and pupils to enter into a spirit of enquiry and through that spirit to establish different styles of teaching and learning. Problem solving cannot be taught. It happens in an environment where skills which have already been acquired are exercised. Indeed, one of its major services is to enable pupils to start from where they are and use whatever they can to make progress. The problems in this book require little in the way of mathematical pre-requisites. Because of this, pupils can always get started and gain something, hence the motivating force of the problems. Nurturing children's curiosity, and developing and refining their spirit of enquiry establishes skills for the future and reasons for learning in the present.

Questioning

Of what does this spirit of enquiry consist? First, and essential, is the existence in the classroom of an atmosphere of *questioning*. Mathematics is frequently presented as the answers to other peoples' questions. Pythagorus was answering an unsolved question when he enunciated his now-famous theorem. Unfortunately, in the codified form in which the answer is taught, the question is lost. Learning answers is a sterile activity if the questions are not yours or do not provide you with a starting point. Pupils often think of questions but are deterred by the pressures of time, syllabus and examinations, and by loss of control, from pursuing them. An atmosphere of questioning is one in which questions are respected for their existence, whether or not we currently know an answer, or even a route towards finding an answer. If they emerge at an inconvenient moment, there are ways of holding on to them, until a time when they can be attacked. A questions board or a questions file in the classroom can be used to collect questions and one period a week could be devoted to exploring some of them. The richness and array of these questions always astonishes teachers, and in tackling them, the teacher can make use of a variety of mathematical concepts. For example, I recall a conversation overheard between two eight-year-olds on the question of 'What is infinity?'. Such a question would provide a good opportunity for a teacher to explore the number system, look at the number line, investigate diminishing fractions, what you will.

Challenging

Second, is the notion of *challenge*. When a teacher provides problems or puzzles as pupil activities, these can be seen as challenges. But it is not only the resource which is a challenge. Arguments should be challenged also so that pupils can distinguish between an argument which satisfies oneself, as opposed to an argument required to satisfy a sceptic! Pupils will happily play the role of sceptic, looking for falsifying examples. For example, the following challenge provokes an interesting exploration of the relationships between area and perimeter:

In a class which had been working on area and circumference of rectangles, six children announced the following:

David: Two rectangles with the same circumference have the same area.
Susan: Two rectangles with the same area have the same circumference.
Guy: Enlarging the circumference of a rectangle always makes the area increase also.
Serge: Enlarging the area of a rectangle always makes the circumference larger.
Brigid: Every rectangle with an area of 36 cm² has a circumference of not less than 24 cm.
Louise: For any rectangle there is another one of equal area but with a larger circumference.

Do you agree or disagree with these children? Explain why.

Figure 4 demonstrates how Debbie, aged 15, found some counter-examples to disprove David's and Susan's statement:

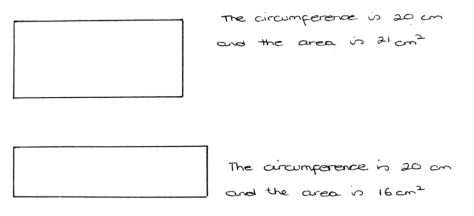

The circumference is 20 cm and the area is 21 cm²

The circumference is 20 cm and the area is 16 cm²

Figure 4

Continued over ▶

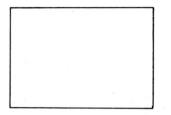

The circumference is 20 cm
and the area is 24 cm²

I disagree with <u>David</u> because the 3 diagrams above all have a circumference of 20cm but the area of all of them vary.

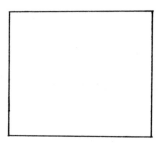

The area is 30 cm²
The circumference is 22cm

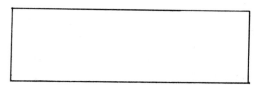

The area is 30 cm²
The circumference is 26 cm

I disagree with <u>Susan</u> because both of the diagrams I have drawn had an ~~circumference~~ area of 30cm² but different circumferences

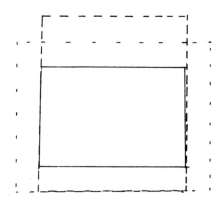

The rectangle has an area of 24cm² and a circumference of 20cm by enlarging the circumference to 28 the area increases to 48cm² (· · · · · ·)
By enlarging the circumference to 26 on the area increase to 42 cm² (– – – –)

Most of her class agreed with Guy. Dionne, also aged 15, put it like this:

What Guy has to say about enlarging the circumference and to make the area bigger is true because the circumference is the outside so obviously if you enlarge the outside the area is bound to get bigger.

However, in another class Katrina and Amanda, aged 11 years, wrote:

Guy is wrong — a rectangle is 15 cm by 5cm
area — 75 cm² circumference — 40cm
if we enlarge the rectangles by 10 cm this happens
rectangle is 24 cm by 1cm
area — 24 cm² circumference — 50cm
but the area is smaller than before.

13

In Figure 5 David, aged 13, used his thinking about David's and Susan's statements to falsify the statements of Guy and Serge.

David. This is false as

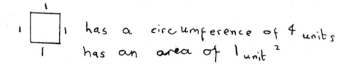

has a circumference of 4 units
has an area of 1 unit²

has a circumference of 4 units
has an area of 0·75 units²

Susan This is false as

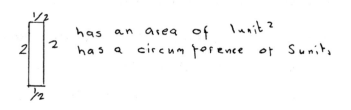

has a circumference of 4 units
has an area of 1 unit²

has an area of 1 unit²
has a circumference of 5 units

Guy This is false as is shown in the example for Susan.

Serge this if false as in Davids explanation the circumfrances are the same but the areas are different

Brigid. This is ~~false~~ True as a 9 by 4 rectangle has an area of ~~39~~ 36 and a circumferance of 26 and a 12 by 3 is 30

Louise This is true as you could get down to almost a straight line.

Figure 5

14

His agreement with Louise's statement is couched in interesting terms which offer the opportunity for a class, or group-based, discussion. David has not tackled the use of 'not less than' in Brigid's statement. He happily validated that statement with two examples. Look at Figures 6 and 7 – the response of another 15-year-old, to the same challenge:

The relation between Circumference and area

area   circumference

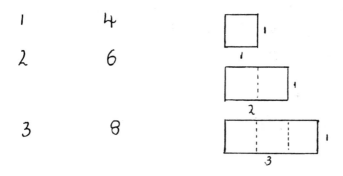

area	circumference
1	4
2	6
3	8

from   this   I   can   see

$$c = 2a + 2$$

so for an area of 100 The Circumference would be 202

BUT what happens when I change the shape

area   circumference

4   8

5   can't be made. into a square of intigers

But The original method would make the circumference 10 for the area 4.

Figure 6

15

so, David is wrong!
and Susan is wrong!
and Guy is Wrong!
and Serge is Wrong!

I think Brigid is write since the smallest circumference seems to be made by a square. and a square with area 36 cm² has a circumference of 24 cm.

Louise is wright aswell, if you don't mind infinitly small sides.

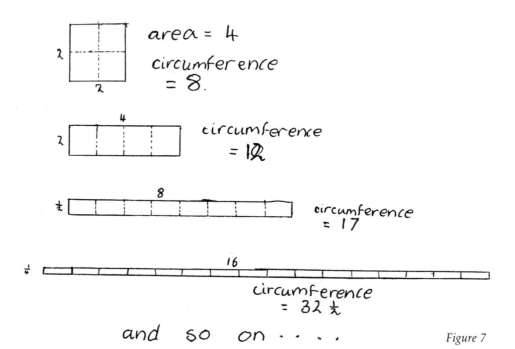

area = 4
circumference = 8.

circumference = 12

circumference = 17

circumference = 32 ¼

and so on . . . .

Figure 7

Discussing meaning, defining terms, exploring the implications of these definitions and critically examining examples are all aspects of enquiry. They cannot be taught. Time is needed to encourage their use and to recognise their utility.

Reflecting

The third component of a classroom in which problem solving is an integral part is an emphasis on *reflection*. If the pupil leaves the processes that are used in tackling a problem at the intuitive level, there is no ready access to them on the next appropriate occasion. The process of Review and Extension therefore includes time to reflect on what was constructive, and what was not, in the Attack on a problem. Comparing the pupil's resolution with others provides an opportunity to reflect on differences in approach or in method. Such reflection deepens the awareness of the pupil's own possibilities as well as expanding his/her repertory of useful procedures.

In a class of six-year-olds, the pupils had used geoboards to make triangles. They described their triangles by reference to co-ordinates; the 'yellow' numbers from 0 to 10 on the x-axis and the red numbers from 0 to 10 on the y-axis. They chose to use a red number followed by a yellow number to describe a point. The teacher used an overhead projector to show the triangle (1,1), (3,2), (2,5) and asked the children to shift the triangle '+4 in red':

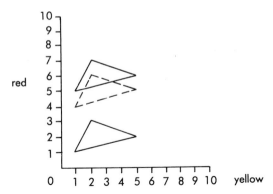

A disagreement ensued between those who thought that the new triangle would have co-ordinates (4,1), (6,2), (5,5) and those who thought that it should be (5,1), (7,2), (6,5). The first group (the majority), interpreted '+4' as 'move 4 points', while the second understood it as 'move 4 intervals'. Some children discovered that it was easier to add 4 to the appropriate co-ordinate. The teacher encouraged the children to explore the consequences of their preferences and to argue out their disagreement until finally all were convinced that the first group had proposed a good response to the instruction '+3 in red' but that the instruction '+4 in red' required the second set of co-ordinates.

The teacher's role is to ensure that reflection is both possible and valued. Questions such as:

'Why do you think that?'

'What difference will that make?'

17

'Is it always so?'

'When is it not so?'

'Can you convince someone else of your point of view?'

'What did you do to arrive at that conclusion?'

'Is there another way of doing that?'

'Is there a better way?'

cause the pupils to examine the procedures which have been used and evaluate them. Thus, they have something positive to recall and apply on a future occasion.

Those who have spent time observing the problem-solving behaviour of pupils note two things. First, problem-solving behaviour is positively affected when the *processes* rather than the outcome, are the focus of attention. Reflecting on the processes and making their use the major reason for the activity not only encourages their use but also improves the pupils' problem-solving performance. Second, when pupils are problem solving they do not call on the level of mathematical skills or knowledge which they are expected to 'know'. For example, pupils who have done some algebra will not necessarily use algebraic skills in solving a problem but may resort to trying simple cases. The level of mathematics learnt does not seem to be the same as the level of mathematics pupils actually use when they are investigating an unfamiliar question. If this is the case, providing opportunities to select and use appropriate mathematics already learned sets that knowledge and skills into a context. It is arguable that being able to use what one knows is of greater value than acquiring more inert knowledge.

Problem solving is usually a group activity where pupils collaborate to pool understanding, knowledge and skills. When a group of pupils works together, the whole is greater than the sum of the parts because of the opportunity to expand perceptions, try different approaches or 'see' something from a new perspective. More will be said of this in Chapter 5.

Why are mathematical explorations and investigations of value in their own right? Because:

1 They enthuse and excite pupils.
2 They provide opportunities for creativity.
3 They can be attacked at various levels of sophistication so everyone can enjoy and achieve something.
4 They build confidence and independence.
5 They develop collaborative learning.
6 They enable pupils to recognise and apply what they already have stored.
7 They shift the focus of attention from what is learned, to how that learning is used.
8 They give meaning and value to the study of mathematics.

3 HOW TO GET GOING

Teacher's choice of problem

Thirty problems are available in Chapter 7, laid out in a way which should help with the choice of which problems suit a particular purpose. The key to the layout is on page 62. For a mathematics club or a problem-solving class, open choice is usually part of the activity and you might prefer to offer a wide range of problems. However, experience does suggest that too many problems can be overwhelming.

Each problem is classified according to its type. It can be a Number problem, a Spatial problem, a Logical problem, a Combinatorics problem or a combination of more than one of these. For example, to make use of all the problems relevant to geometry, look at all those problems classified as Spatial. Where the problem requires making a generalisation, it is in addition classified G. The right-hand page of each problem spread includes the appropriate strategies and skills from the listing of Organising Questions, Procedures and Skills in Chapter 4. These are classified by the relevant problem-solving phases (Entry, Attack and Review-Extension) in which they occur. Problems can therefore be chosen to provide experience with particular procedures or to focus on a particular phase.

Most of the problems can be investigated with a varying degree of sophistication. The same problem can thus be a challenge to solvers of a wide range of both age and ability. Indeed, different responses to a problem can provide an excellent resource in the classroom for extending and deepening particular pupils' thinking. Ideas to help these exchanges will be found in this chapter.

The symbol ▲ will be found in the text with a note alerting you to difficulties which may arise. This will be followed by the symbol ■ with suggestions for overcoming these difficulties.

Pupils' choice of problem

Solvers must have the feeling that the problem 'belongs' to them. To generate this feeling, choice is most important. Observations with pupils confirm that choosing a problem introduces no additional burdens and it does affect attitudes to problem solving positively.

- ▲ check reading level necessary for each problem
- ▲ check logical demands of each problem
- ■ encourage pupils to work together
- ■ challenge pupils to justify to each other their statements or their approaches

Organising the classroom

Different problems tend to be appropriate to different types of classroom organisation. For example, the longer and more complex problems are well-suited to a whole class format where the teacher and pupils are working at the problem together. Shorter, simpler problems tend to be resolved too quickly for whole class participation and are more often used by solvers working in pairs or in small groups. In most classrooms, pupils are offered a choice of problems and are invited to work together at a problem of their choosing. Ample representational materials should be available. Under this structure, teachers find that pupils develop independence, collaborate well and produce inventive and interesting work.

▲ check physical arrangements in classroom
■ re-arrange furniture to facilitate discussion

Some teachers have experimented with a problem corner. For this, one problem is displayed each week but in subsequent weeks previous problems are not removed. In this way an increasing number of problems is available through the term or half-term, and solvers are free to continue working on one problem or to swop to another, as they prefer. This allows variable depth of response to a particular problem. For an example of the work developed by two 11-year-old pupils over half a term on The Milk Crate (Problem 3), see Burton, L., 'Problems and Puzzles', in *For the Learning of Mathematics*.

Another method is to offer pupils a homework problem, which is then discussed in class time so that variations in method or resolution can be compared and assessed. One way of doing this is to display all the resolutions of the homework problem so that pupils can not only make judgments about methods, results and developments, but questions of elegance of resolution can be raised.

Role of the teacher

Solvers must accept responsibility for what they do and how they do it. In this way, they understand and appreciate better the implications of their choices. Under these circumstances the teacher's role shifts from that of providing information, to question-asker and resource-provider. Initially, this should allow solvers to direct their work without any intervention. If they are stuck, some sample interventions which have proved helpful to teachers, are offered on the problem sheets. Teachers should remember that if too much interjection is made, the problem becomes theirs. The reason for the activity will then have been lost.

▲ ask yourself 'Who is doing the thinking?'

- build confidence by expecting pupil autonomy, providing appropriate resources and by asking helpful questions (see below)
- challenge pupils to justify or falsify arguments and to reflect on what has been done

Problem solving cannot be done to order and if the solvers are to be involved with what they are doing, they need to feel free of pressure to finish. It is important, therefore, that the time for problem solving is open-ended in the sense that the problem can be continued in the next session without a feeling that some conclusion must be reached at the end of each session. It is equally important that the solvers feel free to approach their problem in their chosen way and that a feature is made of different approaches. This will increase their creativity and invention.

The Organising Questions associated with each problem help focus and direct the solver's attention (see p.25). They are meant to set the tone of the teacher's interventions by emphasising enquiry rather than instruction. Eventually solvers should acquire the habit of asking themselves such questions.

- ▲ do not assume that questioning happens automatically
- ■ make questioning explicit by repeated reference to the particular organising questions

Role of the solver

Problem-solving habits are important if solvers are to sustain interest, motivation and success. These habits are referred to below as the 'good housekeeping' level of problem solving (p.27). However, there follow three aspects which should be stressed: choosing and using representations, resolving and communicating.

Choosing and using representations

The confidence and ability to model a problem is frequently a key to its solution. It has been encouraging to see how solvers can develop this habit, and how it improves their problem solving, and it is a great pity that many adults feel that representing a problem by a concrete or pictorial method is 'babyish'. It is important, however, that the representation is appropriate to the problem. For example, pupils who model the Milk Crate problem using counters on squared paper often find a solution more easily than those who use a pictorial method, and frequently observe symmetries which encourage interesting extensions.

- ▲ solver 'stuck'
- ■ encourage solvers to use a representation or to change their representation

Resolving rather than solving

The problem-solving process is not a linear one: problem ──────→ solution
but a cyclical one:

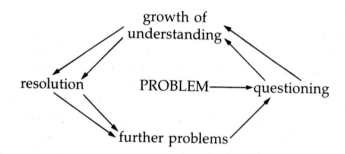

Out of an initial problem and its first resolution, can grow a network of new questions, new resolutions, and further questions. Solvers should be encouraged to develop this attitude. The spiral movement makes the problem-solving process both more interesting and more personal since each solver can choose to focus on different aspects of a resolution in order to ask further questions.

▲ solver 'finished'
■ ask 'What if . . .' questions to encourage extensions (see chapter 7). Try also 'What if not . . .'*

Questions can be collected to form the basis of future problems so that the bank of problems is expanded by the activities of the pupils.

Communicating

Communicating mathematics presents special difficulties. Traditionally, emphasis has been placed on the recording of mathematics in symbols. However, different methods of communication are suitable for different purposes. Two habits should be encouraged:

Keep a record as you go – this record will be informal and personal, either jotted down in pictures, words or symbols, or possibly in concrete form using the apparatus chosen for representing the problem.
Be systematic – structuring the jottings systematically will highlight patterns.

---

* This technique, developed by Stephen Brown and Marion Walter, and delightfully presented in *The Art of Problem Posing*, encourages solvers to change one aspect of a problem statement at a time. Thus, with the problem 'How many squares can you find on an 8 × 8 chessboard?' you might 'not' the squares, and ask 'How many rectangles can you find on an 8 × 8 chessboard?' or you might 'not' the 8 × 8 and ask about a 12 × 12, or an $n \times n$, or you might 'not' the chessboard! Some pupils developed the question: 'How many triangles can be found on a triangular, isometric 8 × 8 × 8 board?'

Pupils should be encouraged to present their findings formally in the final stages of a problem only, when there is a need to inform and to communicate to others what has been done. You could experiment with different forms of communication. For example:

1 *Individual Problem-solving files* in which pupils keep their resolutions.
2 *Problem folder* in which all the resolutions of a particular problem are gathered.
3 *Display board* possibly supported by a cassette tape on which pupils describe and discuss what they have done.
4 *Problem-solving assembly* using overhead projector slides.
5 *Computer file* in which pupils store their resolutions to particular problems.

▲ check sloppy, imprecise presentation of results
▲ who is the solver informing, and of what?
■ check that the solver accepts the reasons for communicating

Finally, remember we learn from non-verbal behaviour as well as from verbal interactions. If your pupils never see you engaged in problem solving, they will learn that despite what goes on in your classroom, it is not an activity which is important to *you*. Provide your pupils with a model for problem-solving behaviour by making sure that sometimes they see you attempting problems. Share these attempts with them in the same way in which you ask them to share their attempts with you. Plan for time when you and the pupils solve problems together.

4 THE PROBLEM-SOLVING PROCESS

Four phases of activity can be observed during the process of solving a problem. These are referred to as Entry, Attack, Review and Extension.

Entry

The solver, having received the problem, is trying to understand what it is about and clarify what must be done. It is during this phase that choosing and using a representation form is important. If the problem is couched in general terms, looking at particular examples in concrete or pictorial form may well provide the necessary impetus to move into the next phase. The progression is signalled by an emotional change in the solver who begins to feel ready to undertake more substantial work.

Attack

The major activity of finding a resolution to the problem takes place in this phase. A resolution will not be found immediately, and the solver will be stuck, once or many times. The Organising Questions and the Procedures listed below are designed to suggest possible ways of dealing with being stuck. Sometimes, the solver will need to return to the Entry phase in order to re-assess the direction which was taken.
Note: recognising that one is stuck is the first step to overcoming it. Being stuck is good so long as one has access to actions that will help. Recognising a way out of the problem after being stuck is always accompanied by a feeling of euphoria (Aha!), even if it transpires that the 'solution' wasn't so helpful after all!

Review

This phase begins when the solver feels that the essence of a resolution has been achieved. Now is the time to examine the resolution and, if it is found to be inadequate the process returned to the Entry or Attack stage. It is during this phase that the resolution is written up so that it can be understood by others. This encourages checking, exercises communication skills, suggests further questions to ask and generally draws together what has been done.

Extension

Problem solving is a continuous process, since every resolution of a problem can lead on to further problems. Most problems have embedded within them the seeds of new problems and part of the excitement of mathematical enquiry is developing these seeds. Extension helps to reinforce significant features of the resolution of the original problem and can be particularly useful in ensuring that a review is conducted. Sometimes it highlights errors which may otherwise have been overlooked in the original resolution. Review and Extension are interrelated and for convenience, are treated together in describing the stages of problem solving. Successful Extension leads to the adoption of a new problem and the spiralling process of Entry, Attack, Review and Extension begins again.

A feature of the behaviour of experienced problem solvers is their possession of a repertory of useful strategies, general and specific, which guide and inform their problem-solving behaviour at any given moment. These strategies operate at different levels.

Organising Questions

These questions focus the attention of the problem solver partly by providing a goal for which to aim and partly by aiding the recall of associated Procedures. The use of an Organising Question explains to some extent why the procedures with which it is associated are helpful.

Entry

1.1 What does the problem tell me?
1.2 What does the problem ask me?
1.3 What can I introduce to help get started?

Attack

2.1 Can I make connections?
2.2 Is there a result which will help?
2.3 Is there a pattern?
2.4 Can I discover how or why?
2.5 Can I break down the problem?
2.6 Can I change my view of the problem?

Review-Extension

3.1 Is the resolution acceptable?
3.2 What can I learn from the resolution?
3.3 Can I extend the resolution?

Procedures

These are independent of the subject matter of the problem. They exhort the solver to move in a particular direction but it is through experience in problem solving that the necessary connections are made. For example, P2.8: Try related problems encourages the solver to transform the current problem into a more accessible, but related, problem. So a problem related to Leapfrog (Problem 19) would be to use one red and one black counter on a row of three squares.

Entry

1.1   Explore the problem
1.2   Make and test guesses
1.3   Define terms and relationships
1.4   Extract information
1.5   Organise the information
1.6   Introduce a representation
1.7   Introduce a form of recording

Attack

2.0   Be systematic
2.1   Search for relationships
2.2   Analyse relationships
2.3   Make simplifying assumptions
2.4   Find properties the answer will have
2.5   Try particular cases
2.6   Adjust guesses
2.7   Formulate and test hypotheses
2.8   Try related problems
2.9   Control variables systematically
2.10   Use one solution to find others
2.11   Work backwards
2.12   Focus on one aspect of the problem
2.13   Eliminate paths
2.14   Partition the problem into cases
2.15   Reformulate the problem
2.16   Upset set
2.17   Develop the recording system
2.18   Change the representation
2.19   Make a generalisation

Review-Extension

3.1   Check
3.2   Look back
3.3   Communicate
3.4   Find isomorphic problems
3.5   Extend to a class of problems
3.6   Create different problems

Skills

These are not as powerful in problem solving as the Procedures. None the less they are necessary for, or at least helpful in, the resolution of some problems. Many skills, for example that of choosing and using a flow chart as a representational form, are taught as part of the mathematics curriculum. However, curriculum content is not always seen to be appropriate or relevant to problems outside the immediate mathematics curriculum. This is another reason for making time for problem solving, as it offers opportunities for the application of such knowledge or skills.

Skills for handling information

1.1 Identifying information
1.2 Collecting information
1.3 Recording information
1.4 Sorting and ordering
1.5 Presenting information

Skills for representing a problem

2.1 Choosing a mode
2.2 Using a representation
2.3 Translating between representations

Skills for enumerating

3.1 Scanning all possibilities
3.2 Eliminating needless repetition

Skills for finding patterns

4.1 Recognising patterns
4.2 Predicting from a pattern

Skills for testing

5.1 Testing a result
5.2 Testing a hypothesis
5.3 Testing an argument

Good housekeeping

Successful problem solvers exhibit features of an effective working method. These features are tactics which aid problem solving although they are not essential to it. Such tactics become good habits which should be practised rather than taught, although their adoption will be affected by the teacher clearly modelling their use.

It is helpful to have your material ready – lots of paper, sharp pencils, rubbers and so on. When you have a good idea, write yourself a message, then you won't forget what you did and how you did it; don't turn over your paper – take a new sheet; number each page as you go.

Pupils are taught mathematics explicitly but are expected to acquire enquiry skills, attitudes and habits indirectly. This expectation is rarely fulfilled partly because real enquiry is often lacking in the mathematics classroom and partly because the processes of enquiry are left as part of the hidden curriculum. For pupils to become more proficient problem solvers, these processes must be recognised and featured as part of the repertory of behaviours natural to all good problem solvers. Reminders – either by using the Organising Questions, or by referring directly to the Procedures, will aid the pupils in recognising the tools they already possess and in extending their range.

There follows a detailed description of the Organising Questions, the Procedures and the Skills. Pupils should be encouraged to adopt these in some form.

Organising Questions for Entry

O1.1 *What does the problem tell me?*
This procedure directs attention to examining the information given in the problem in order to extract all of it and to understand and become familiar with it.

Useful procedures: P1.1, P1.3, P1.4, P1.5

O1.2 *What does the problem ask me?*
Here attention is directed to clarifying exactly what the problem requires, including identifying knowns and unknowns and distinguishing the unknowns which have to be found.

Useful procedures: P1.1, P1.2, P1.3, P1.4

O1.3 *What can I introduce to help get started?*
This procedure directs attention to those elements which are not given in the problem but which the solver has to introduce in order to find a resolution. Examples are concrete representations, diagrams and graphs, symbols, mechanisms for recording results and tables and charts.

Useful procedures: P1.3, P1.5, P1.6, P1.7

Organising Questions for Attack

O2.1 *Can I make connections?*
This directs attention to searching for links between variables or between different aspects of the problem. Relationships can be

uncovered from the information given about the problem, deduced from other relationships or hypothesised and then checked.

Useful procedures: P2.1, P2.2, P2.7, P2.17, P2.19

O2.2 *Is there a result which will help?*
This directs attention to the setting of subgoals, finding accessible features of the solution or even finding results which can be modified or adapted to give a solution. The information found may be of direct benefit or may help indirectly by providing extra information.

Useful procedures: P2.1, P2.3, P2.4, P2.5, P2.6

O2.3 *Is there a pattern?*
Patterns abound in mathematics. Finding and then exploiting a pattern is an important device of wide application.

Useful procedures: P2.0, P2.1, P2.5, P2.7, P2.8, P2.9, P2.10, P2.17, P2.19

O2.4 *Can I discover how or why?*
This procedure encourages the development of insight into methods which may resolve the problem.

Useful procedures: P2.0, P2.5, P2.8, P2.10, P2.11

O2.5 *Can I break down the problem?*
It is often convenient to attack a problem one piece at a time, possibly dealing with separate pieces in different ways.

Useful procedures: P2.0, P2.9, P2.12, P2.13, P2.14

O2.6 *Can I change my view of the problem?*
This directs attention to finding a new way of looking at the problem and adopting a fresh approach. This may take the solver back into the Entry stage or produce either a radically different or merely reformulated view of the problem.

Useful procedures: P2.15, P2.16, P2.17, P2.18

Organising Questions for Review-Extension

O3.1 *Is the resolution acceptable?*
This question directs attention not only to the correctness or otherwise of the answer obtained but also to whether or not it, or

the method by which it was obtained, can be improved. The term 'acceptable' is used instead of 'correct' to cater for the large class of problems involving mathematical modelling for which there is no 'correct' answer but a range of acceptable ones.

Useful procedures: P3.1, P3.2, P3.3

O3.2 *What can I learn from the resolution?*
A careful review of a resolution can teach a solver about both content and process. This benefit is not only obtained by looking back but also by trying to extend the resolution and so looking forward.

Useful procedures: P3.2, P3.3, P3.4, P3.5

O3.3 *Can I extend the resolution?*
Extending resolutions is beneficial because it highlights and places in context significant aspects of both the content and the process of the resolution. Extension encourages creativity, independence and interest.

Useful procedures: P3.4, P3.5, P3.6

Procedures for Entry

P1.1 *Explore the problem*
Associated Organising Questions: O1.1, O1.2

This procedure involves getting the feel of the problem by playing around or juggling with the data or information given in the problem.

Examples
i) In Problem 28, one could explore the problem by finding one or two possible routes for the fly.
ii) In Problem 20, one could explore by writing down a few of the signposts and seeing how many digits they used.

P1.2 *Make and test guesses*
Associated Organising Question: O1.2

In this procedure an initial guess is made at the solution to the problem.

Examples
i) In Problem 9, one could consider what happens if there are 10 people and each has one cake and one cup of tea.

ii) In Problem 9, one could consider what happens if each person has one cake and one cup of tea.

iii) In Problem 19, one could attempt a solution making arbitrary decisions whenever necessary.

P1.3   *Define terms and relationships*
Associated Organising Questions: O1.1, O1.2, O1.3

The problem should be examined to make sure that the meaning of each term used is understood and that the relationships given in the problem are understood. Some useful techniques here are to closely examine a specific case which exemplifies a definition and to draw a diagram to exhibit relationships.

Examples
i) In Problem 10, the term 'perfect' must be understood.
ii) In Problem 27, the meaning of 'different' must be decided.
iii) In Problem 25, the relationships must be examined at the Entry stage.

P1.4   *Extract information*
Associated Organising Questions: O1.1, O1.2

The problem is examined carefully to extract all the information supplied.

Examples
i) In Problem 19, information must be extracted about the way the red counters are allowed to move, the way the black counters are allowed to move and the starting and finishing positions.
ii) In Problem 12, many pieces of information are given and they are stated both positively and negatively.

P1.5   *Organise the information*
Associated Organising Questions: O1.1, O1.3

The information given in the problem should be taken and sorted into a usable form. Categories should be chosen and information arranged accordingly, putting information in order of time or importance. Useful techniques involve constructing tables and drawing diagrams.

Examples
i) In Problem 12, the written information can be sorted by using a table.
ii) In Problem 24, pictorial information has to be sorted and classified. If a table is constructed showing which faces are known to be adjacent, then the problem is almost solved.

31

P1.6 *Introduce a representation*
Associated Organising Question: O1.3

A concrete, pictorial or symbolic representation could be introduced to use during Entry and Attack stages. The representation
may be chosen from known representations or a special representation may be constructed. The representation may later be modified or abandoned.

Examples
i) A concrete representation is introduced in Problem 5 by the
child who makes a grill out of plasticine and uses small pieces of
paper as bread.
ii) A symbolic representation is introduced in Problem 1 if the
variables are named and an algebraic formulation of the problem is
used.

P1.7 *Introduce a form of recording*
Associated Organising Question: O1.3

A notation or other means can be introduced to record the steps of
the resolution or the information obtained. This mechanism may
have to be modified or radically altered in the Attack phase (see
P2.17).

Example
In Problem 4, before any progress can be made, the solver needs a
way of indicating where the men are and have been, and how
much food is left.

Procedures for Attack

P2.0 *Be systematic*
Associated Organising Questions: O2.3, O2.4, O2.5

A systematic approach to the investigation should be adopted.
This procedure appears first because it is different in nature from
the others. It is frequently the key to the successful use of other
procedures and skills.

Examples
i) In Problem 10, numbers can be tested (using P2.5) to see if they
are perfect either randomly or systematically.
ii) A hypothesis may be formulated (using P2.7) either by systematically examining a number of particular cases, or alternatively
by looking at one individual case.

iii) A path may be eliminated (using P2.13), accidentally, by using a piece of information that has been discovered or systematically, by listing the possible paths and examining each in turn.

P2.1 *Search for relationships*
Associated Organising Questions: O2.1, O2.2, O2.3

The mathematical relationships can be abstracted from the given situation and a search for relationships between variables be made. Although this procedure is carried out to some extent in the Entry phase, a deeper search is often necessary.

Examples
i) In Problem 9, the total bill is given by relating the number of people to the cost per head. This will arise in the Entry phase for some solvers, but in the Attack phase for others.
ii) In Problem 24 the opposite faces of a cube are those that are not adjacent.
iii) Problem 26 requires four relationships to be found.

P2.2 *Analyse relationships*
Associated Organising Question: O2.1

Relationships are analysed by logical argument or mathematical technique to see what the consequences are.

Examples
i) Problem 17 is solved by analysing the relationships between the dimensions of the faces of a rectangular box.
ii) A solver who has identified the relationships represented by A, B, C and D in Problem 26 can analyse them to explain why their combined effect is to reduce the starting number.

P2.3 *Make simplifying assumptions*
Associated Organising Question: O2.2

Variables can be chosen without losing generality, often by using the symmetry of the situation or by choosing particular scaling factors or orientations.

Examples
i) In Problem 29, one can make the first face of the bigger cube arbitrarily (provided each colour is used).
ii) In Problem 19, one can assume that the first counter to move is red.

P2.4 *Find properties the answer will have*
Associated Organising Question: O2.2

Accessible features of the solution can be found that may later be useful in actually finding the solution, even if the information gained is not directly relevant.

Examples
i) In Problem 1, since the number of rabbits must be even, the number of hutches is odd and the numbers involved must be small.
ii) In Problem 15, one can argue by comparing the area of the base of the box and the tray that there can be at most 36 boxes on the tray.

P2.5 *Try particular cases*
Associated Organising Questions: O2.2, O2.3, O2.4

Detailed consideration can be given to particular cases obtained by adding extra constraints to the problem. Some or all of the variables could be given numerical values or a special relationship may be imposed between variables, such as looking at limiting cases or assuming one variable is a multiple of another.

Examples
i) In Problem 10, trying to find perfect numbers could be done by testing numbers individually.
ii) In Problem 10, the particular case of numbers which are powers of 2 could be settled because their factors are known.
iii) In Problem 15, one could consider the two cases where all the boxes have the same orientation.

P2.6 *Adjust guesses*
Associated Organising Question: O2.2

This is a trial and error procedure where there is a plan for selecting the next 'trial' on the basis of the 'errors' which have been observed. Iterative methods such as Newton's method for solving equations are highly refined examples of this procedure.

Example
In Problem 14, a child could choose any numerical value for the width as a first trial and then adjust this value up or down according to whether the corresponding perimeter is less or more than 28 cm. Provided a record of the trials is kept, the problem can be solved quite efficiently in this manner.

P2.7   *Formulate and test hypotheses*
Associated Organising Questions: O2.1, O2.3

In this procedure data is gathered, arranged systematically and examined for patterns. When a pattern is spotted it is formulated as a hypothesis which is then tested against further evidence.

Example
In Problem 8, the child may construct a table showing number of streets and maximum number of lamp-posts required and notice that the difference between successive numbers increases steadily by one.

P2.8   *Try related problems*
Associated Organising Questions: O2.3, O2.4

A related problem is selected and solved in the hope that either the results obtained or the methods used may be exploited to help solve the original problem. The related problem may be a smaller-scale version of the original problem (say with fewer variables or smaller parameters), it may be obtained by altering some of the constraints of the original problem or it may be a rather different problem recalled because the solver suspects it may have used the same techniques of solution or required a similar insight.

Examples
i) In Problem 5, the problem of the grill can be tried with two spaces (as suggested) before the grill with 3 spaces.
ii) Trying to solve problem 21 with a well only 3 m deep.
Note: Many of the problems in Chapter 7 are phrased so as to encourage children to use this procedure.

P2.9   *Control variables systematically*
Associated Organising Questions: O2.3, O2.5

Where there are several variables, all but one are held constant whilst the effect of systematic variation of the other is observed. Different values of the constant variables should be considered. Each variable is examined in turn.

Example
In Problem 6, the case-by-case consideration can be done, using this procedure.

P2.10　*Use one solution to find others*
Associated Organising Questions: O2.3, O2.4

Once a solution has been found either the information gained in finding it can be used to search for other solutions or the solution itself can be modified to give others.

Examples
i) In Problem 13, a child who has constructed two towers of equal height (with 11 cubes) can swap some cubes from one tower to the other to get more solutions.
ii) A child who has one solution to Problem 29, can permute the colours to obtain other solutions.

P2.11　*Work backwards*
Associated Organising Question: O2.4

When an answer is known, one can work backwards step by step, to try to see why it is correct and therefore how to derive it. This procedure is particularly useful when one is asked to show how a complicated result follows from a simple one.

Example
This procedure is not well illustrated in Chapter 7 because the problems do not offer something to prove. However, a child who accidentally hits upon an answer, say to Problem 24 or 29 may be able to analyse why his answer is correct and thereby discover how to do the problem without guesswork.

P2.12　*Focus on one aspect of the problem*
Associated Organising Question: O2.5

When a problem is clearly made up of separate parts, it may help to look at one part at a time and resolve each before combining the results to resolve the whole problem.

Examples
i) In Problem 4, one could first of all concentrate on the aspect of burying food and find out how much food can be buried at each place. After this is done, one can consider how the men can actually use the food.
ii) This procedure is most useful in problems which are longer than those in Chapter 7, especially in real-life problems.

P2.13 *Eliminate paths*
Associated Organising Question: O2.5

Possibilities can be considered and eliminated if they lead to contradictions or are otherwise seen to be impossible.

Examples
i) In Problem 24, one can find the pattern opposite S by considering the other five symbols in turn and eliminating all but one with the given views of the cube.
ii) In Problem 23, at each stage one can consider all legal moves and eliminate all but one on the grounds that the move would not change the situation (e.g. the person who rows across must immediately row back) or that the move would return the situation to an earlier stage.

P2.14 *Partition the problem into cases*
Associated Organising Question: O2.5

The problem is split into a number of subproblems each of which is attacked separately. Each subproblem should be easier to solve than the original problem because there is more information to work with. When all the subproblems have been completed they will provide a complete resolution to the problem.

Examples
i) In Problem 5, the general problem of grilling *n* pieces of bread on a grill which takes two slices could be divided into the two cases of *n* even and *n* odd.
ii) The method of attack given for Problem 6 is an extreme example of this method. All possible combinations of rods are systematically listed and separately tested to see what type of triangle (if any) can be formed.
iii) In Problem 16, a child wanting to find all nets for a cube divided the problem into three cases where there were 4 squares in a row, at most 3 squares in a row and at least 2 squares in a row.

P2.15 *Reformulate the problem*
Associated Organising Question: O2.6

The problem may be presented in a different way to make it clearer to the individual solving the problem, or may be moulded into a different format which is more amenable to solution. Useful techniques include changing representation or notation or arguing by contradiction or using the contrapositive.

Examples
i) Trying to arrange the six spaces instead of the 18 milk bottles in Problem 3.
ii) Problem 27 can be reformulated into a problem of finding the number of ways a given number can be written as the product of three integers.

P2.16 *Upset set*
Associated Organising Question: O2.6

Preconceived ideas about the problem which are wrong or unhelpful can be removed. It may be possible to break out from a restrictive idea of how to solve the problem, or to fundamentally change the view of the problem.

Example
In Problem 8, the set may be thinking that streets must cross at right angles.

P2.17 *Develop the recording system*
Associated Organising Questions: O2.1, O2.3, O2.6

A way of recording can be developed that is sufficiently concise and comprehensive and which highlights features which appear to be important to the resolution.

Example
In Problem 19, it is necessary to have an efficient system for recording where the counters have been in order to find the minimum number of moves and to find a pattern in the moves.

P2.18 *Change the representation*
Associated Organising Question: O2.6

During the Attack phase it may be found that a representation introduced earlier needs improvement or that new forms of representation can profitably be used instead of, or in addition to, existing ones.

Examples
i) In Problem 8, a pupil may begin by sketching the streets and later try various forms of concrete representation such as rulers and drinking straws for streets. Results for a larger number of streets may be found using both concrete and pictorial representations together. The results may be recorded symbolically.
ii) In Problem 27, a child may begin using cubes and then proceed to represent the rectangular boxes by their dimensions alone.

P2.19 *Make a generalisation*
    Associated Organising Questions: O2.1, O2.3

    One can discover what happens in the general case then express
    the discovery.

    Examples
      i) In Problem 17, one can find the way in which the dimensions
    of the faces of a rectangular box are related.
      ii) In Problem 8, one can find the relationship between the num-
    ber of streets and the greatest number of lamp-posts needed, i.e.
    n streets may require $\frac{1}{2}n\,(n-1)$ lamp-posts.

Procedures for Review-Extension

P3.1 *Check*
    Associated Organising Question: O3.1

    There are two aspects of checking which are specifically related to
    problem solving, rather than to good mathematical technique.
    These are:
    a) Checking that the solution obtained does indeed satisfy the
    conditions given in the problem.
    b) Checking the logic of the argument to make sure, for example,
    that all cases have been considered or that a reformulation of the
    problem has not in fact altered it.

P3.2 *Look back*
    Associated Organising Questions: O3.1, O3.2

    In this procedure the problem may be developed by looking back
    over the resolution and searching for interesting and informative
    features by asking:
    a) Have all the solutions been found?
    b) Can the solution be improved by finding a better answer or a
    more elegant argument?
    c) What was the crucial step in the argument?
    d) Has all the information given in the problem been used?
    e) Is the solution realistic or satisfactory from a practical point of
    view? If not, how should the model used be altered? This aspect of
    looking back is particularly important for solving problems from
    'real life'.

P3.3 *Communicate*
Associated Organising Questions: O3.1, O3.2

The resolution may be put into a form so that others can understand it. This is an important problem-solving procedure because it encourages checking, looking back and extension. All the problems in Chapter 7 require this and it often results in an improvement to the original resolution.

P3.4 *Find isomorphic problems*
Associated Organising Questions: O3.2, O3.3

This involves discovering problems which look different but have exactly the same mathematical structure. Once a problem has been resolved, one may find a whole class of problems which may be resolved in a similar way.

Examples
i) One may see that the resolution to Problem 5 (Making Toast) can be applied to the class of problems involving machines which act on one side of the object inserted but can deal with two or more objects at once.
ii) One may realise that Problem 13 is essentially the same if the cubes are replaced by rods, strips of squared paper or numbers.

P3.5 *Extend to a class of problems*
Associated Organising Questions: O3.2, O3.3

The problem may be changed by allowing some fixed data in the problem to take arbitrary values. The given problem is then a member of this extended class of problems. The individual problems of the class will have related, but not necessarily similar, solutions.

Examples
i) The number of cubes used in Problem 13 may be varied.
ii) In Problem 19 one could vary the number of counters and the size of the board.

P3.6 *Create different problems*
Associated Organising Question: O3.3

Some of the ideas involved in the original problem may be used but new ideas or constraints may be introduced, old constraints relaxed. The solution to the original problem may not be related in any way to the solution of the new problem.

Examples
i) Problem 8 could be changed by insisting that any pair of streets is either parallel or perpendicular.
ii) The number of fours that can be used in Problem 22 could be restricted.
iii) In Problem 2, one could find the product or sum of the divisors instead of their number.

Skills for handling information

S1.1 *Identifying information*
One could extract all the information from the statement of the problem. The skills involved here are principally reading skills (see Kalmykova, J. (ed.), 'Coping with Word Problems: Observations of V.D. Petrova's class', in Floyd, A. (ed.), *Developing Mathematical Thinking*, pp.186–192).

Examples
i) In Problem 12, the solver has to use information presented verbally and both positively and negatively.
ii) In problems 24 and 25, the information is presented visually.

S1.2 *Collecting information*
Data or further information can be obtained by mathematical processes such as substituting numerical values, or by other processes such as constructing a questionnaire or consulting a dictionary.

Example
In Problem 2, information about the divisors that numbers have is collected by trying numbers systematically.

S1.3 *Recording information*
Information that has been gathered can be recorded either pictorially or symbolically (perhaps even concretely).

Examples
i) In Problem 19, it is necessary to record the moves of the counters on paper in order to make progress with the problem.
ii) In Problem 2, the number of divisors of each number tested should be recorded in a table.
iii) Devices such as the five-bar gate, ﾊﾊﾑ are useful to record results of surveys, etc.

S1.4 *Sorting and ordering*
Information should be arranged systematically so that it can be analysed or presented to others. Tables, charts and graphs can be constructed to show significant aspects of the information.

Example
In Problem 12, a table showing the days on which each person is free to play badminton can be constructed.

S1.5 *Presenting information*
An idea can be expressed with words, diagrams or pictures. The process by which a resolution was found should be clearly explained. A mathematical argument should be written logically so that it is complete and comprehensible. These skills apply in all areas of the curriculum.

Example
Reporting on what has been done in any problem, whether a correct resolution has or has not been obtained, requires these skills of expression.

Skills for representing a problem

S2.1 *Choosing a mode*
It may be decided to represent the problem in a pictorial mode (e.g. using a graph), a concrete mode (e.g. using Cuisenaire rods), or in a symbolic mode (e.g. algebraically).

Example
A child doing Problem 23 can choose a concrete representation (say rods) for the men, the boys and the canoe, can draw pictures to represent each stage or can work with symbols, using MM–BB, for example, to represent a stage where the men are on one side of the river and the boys are on the other.

S2.2 *Using a representation*
The problem should be related to the chosen representation and the representation may be manipulated.

Example
The skills of drawing and interpreting graphs are required for Problem 21 to be solved graphically.

S2.3 *Translating between representations*
The use of two representations in one problem requires the skills of translation from one to the other.

Examples
i) Most problems are initially presented linguistically so translation from the linguistic mode to another is often required.
ii) In Problem 21, a child will often begin with a concrete representation and then change to a pictorial or diagrammatic one which is easier to work with.

Skills for enumerating

S3.1　*Scanning all possibilities*
All the cases which have to be considered should be listed systematically.

Examples
i) Problem 16 requires identification of all the places the lid may go.
ii) Problem 6 involves the skill of systematically listing all the subsets of three items from twelve.

S3.2　*Eliminating needless repetition*
One should be able to recognise when two situations are essentially the same and therefore do not require separate analysis.

Example
Problems 29 and 16 can be simplified by using symmetry considerations.

Skills for finding patterns

In addition to the skills S1.2, S1.3, S1.4, the following skills are required for finding patterns.

S4.1　*Recognising patterns*
A simple pattern should be recognised once it is presented in a systematic way. For example, a number pattern may be recognised from a table or patterns of permutations or symmetries such as reflections and rotations may be found.

Examples
i) Problem 26 requires the recognition of four simple patterns: doubling, halving, adding 4 and subtracting 10.
ii) Problem 8 requires the recognition of the pattern of triangular numbers: 1, 3, 6, 10 . . .

S4.2   *Predicting from a pattern*
It may be possible to predict the next term or any specified later term. This skill is important for testing that the right pattern has been found and also for exploiting the pattern to give more results.

Example
Problems 5, 8 and 26 require this skill for testing the result obtained and finding a general result.

Skills for testing

S5.1   *Testing a result*
This involves seeing if a result (guessed or calculated) actually does satisfy the conditions specified in the problem, and is a skill required in all problems.

S5.2   *Testing a hypothesis*
This involves seeing if a general relationship or pattern that has been guessed or induced is likely to be true.

Example
In Problem 8, when the pattern of triangular numbers has been induced from the information given, another result is predicted and independently tested by counting intersections.

S5.3   *Testing an argument*
An argument is checked to see that it is logically correct, its assumptions are justified and that it covers all cases. Using falsification and examining the implications to be drawn from the argument are possible ways.

Example
In Problem 13, the reasoning which explains why building the towers is impossible should be examined, and a check made that no possibilities have been missed.

5 WHAT ABOUT INDIVIDUAL DIFFERENCES?

Here is a problem of the kind that many pupils enjoy:

4   5   .   .   8

Fill in the dots so that this five-figure number can be divided by nine without a remainder.

Figure 8 shows the work of two 12-year-old low-ability pupils, Karen and Denise.

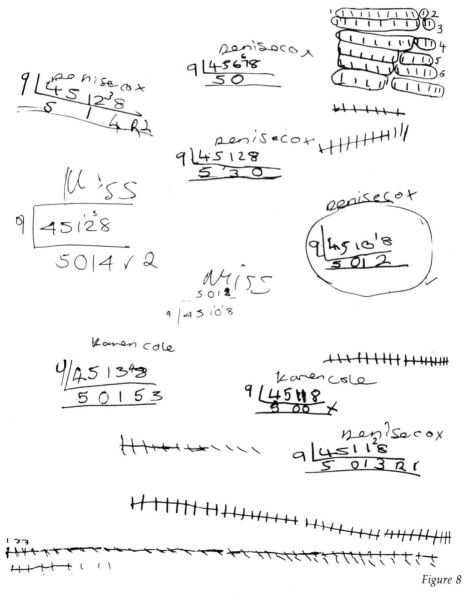

Figure 8

45

Note how they have provided themselves with counting devices. It would have been interesting to see how much further they would have gone if a calculator had been available. Their single solution, 45 108, might then have set them off on a more productive line of attack without the tedium of drawing counting lines.

By comparison, Figure 9 is the work of an able 10-year-old in a primary school:

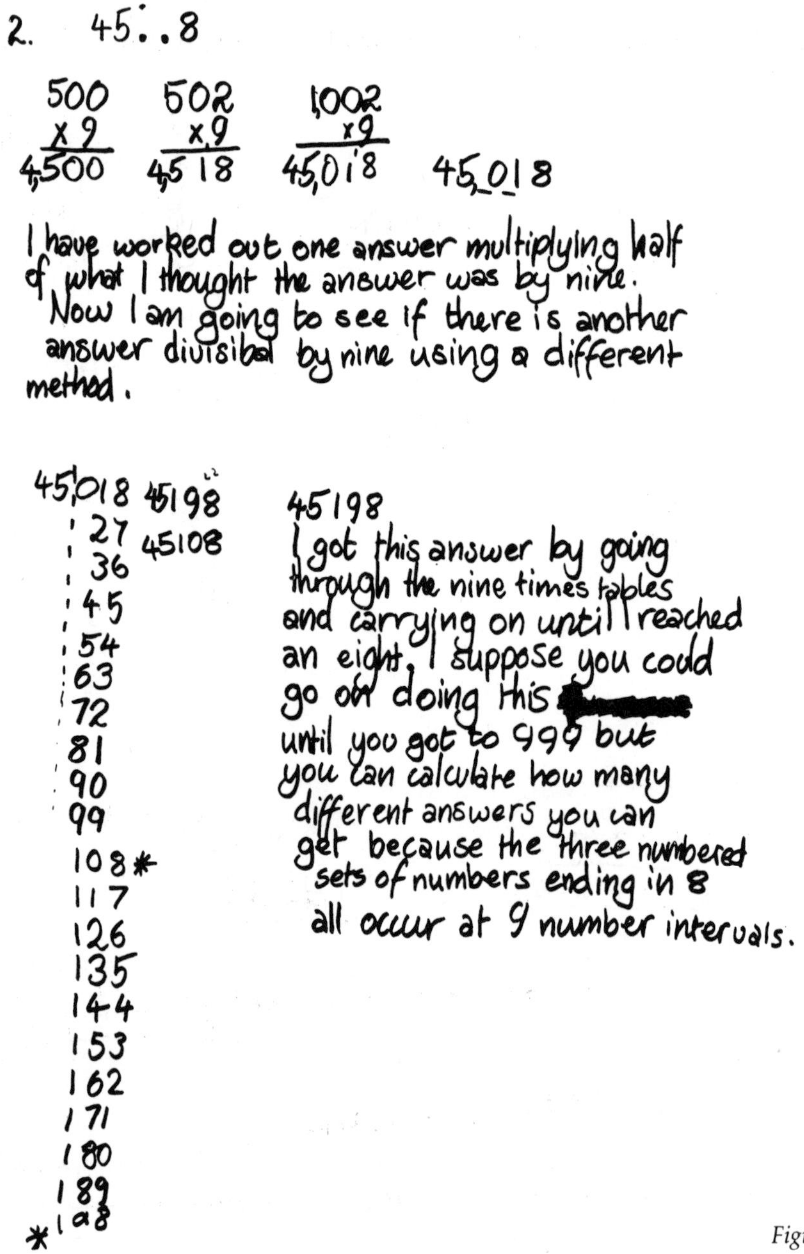

2.   45:..8

$$\begin{array}{c} 500 \\ \times 9 \\ \hline 4,500 \end{array} \qquad \begin{array}{c} 502 \\ \times 9 \\ \hline 4,518 \end{array} \qquad \begin{array}{c} 1,002 \\ \times 9 \\ \hline 45,018 \end{array} \qquad 45,018$$

I have worked out one answer multiplying half of what I thought the answer was by nine. Now I am going to see if there is another answer divisibal by nine using a different method.

45,018   45198
 27   45108
 36
 45
 54
 63
 72
 81
 90
 99
 108*
 117
 126
 135
 144
 153
 162
 171
 180
 189
*108

45198

I got this answer by going through the nine times tables and carrying on until I reached an eight. I suppose you could go on doing this ~~until~~ until you got to 999 but you can calculate how many different answers you can get because the three numbered sets of numbers ending in 8 all occur at 9 number intervals.

Figure 9

46

The responses of these pupils demonstrate why problem solving is a relevant activity for all pupils, whatever their individual level of attainment. The problems in this book have been used by pupils of all abilities, in mixed classes as well as those that are in ability sets. The differences in ability became obvious, as with the above work, in the quality of response *not* in the acceptability of the challenge nor the commitment to it. No teacher had to stop the work because of inattention, poor behaviour or poor motivation. Nor were there signs of any pupils being bored by a challenge which was easily overcome. However, the interest and involvement in problem solving of pupils at all levels of attainment does depend upon certain criteria operating in the classroom.

Pupil choice

Reference to pupil choice has already been made in Chapter 3. Pupils need to find out that they *can* succeed so that there is a decided shift in their confidence and their self-image. This is particularly necessary for less able pupils who have a long history of failure to overcome. Pupil choice, and the decision as to where it is acceptable to reject a problem, no questions asked, gives pupils autonomy over their own actions and respects their ability to exercise that autonomy. More able pupils also need to engage with a problem, since the depth to which they work is likely to depend upon how they develop the problem. So pupil choice is important at all levels of ability.

Working in groups

In order that all pupils can maximise their knowledge, skills and approaches, problem solving is most suitable for groups of pupils working together. Teachers who have moved away from class texts to a use of individualised schemes are increasingly aware of the gains these bring, but also the losses. The freedom for individual pupils to move at their own pace is a considerable gain. The major loss is in the communication between pupils and with the teacher of what is being done and why. Discussion is central to a sharpening of an otherwise 'fuzzy' understanding as well as to the presentation of alternatives. One pupil responding to a question from a teacher leaves the other pupils largely untouched. Each pupil needs to articulate his or her own understanding, listen to how it sounds, and watch how it is received. This can only happen if pupils are discussing and monitoring their own work, as described by Harlen, Darwin and Murphy in *Match and Mismatch*, p.27: 'When two or more children come together, willing to share ideas and effort in a joint venture, they invariably achieve something of much greater worth than they might have done alone.'

In mathematics classrooms using a class text or an individualised scheme approach, problem solving therefore, provides a much-needed time for group exploration and discussion. The advantages quickly become apparent:

1 The pupils accustom themselves to others influencing their mathematical thinking and to their affecting the mathematical thinking of others.
2 The pupils learn to co-operate in planning and executing an enquiry.
3 Different members of the group are valued for different skills.
4 The sharing, refining and developing of good ideas is much richer than is possible if an individual works alone.
5 Meaning is negotiated with one another and also with the teacher.
6 Mathematics is re-viewed, particularly when different approaches to a problem make apparent that a single right method, or a single right answer, are not the norm. If a right answer exists, we can look for the constraints which define its existence. For example, in the problem with which this chapter began, the right answers

  45,018   45,108   45,198 etc.

depend upon calculations in base 10. The rather tedious method demonstrated by the 10-year-old pupil could be affected by a recognition that, in base 10, the digits of numbers divisible by 9, add to 9. So, 18 is divisible by 9, and $1 + 8 = 9$; 27 is divisible by 9, and $2 + 7 = 9$. Setting out the number pattern for 9 to display how this works is usually all that is required to enable children to remember the table of 9. In the case of the problem, the digits of 45 . . 8 add to 8; i.e. $4 + 5 + 8 = 17, 1 + 7 = 8$, so the two gaps can only be filled by pairs of digits which add to 1, since $8 + 1 = 9$.

e.g. $0 + 1 = 1$
$1 + 9 = 10, 1 + 0 = 1$
$7 + 3 = 10, 1 + 0 = 1$
and so on.

An extension of this problem could investigate under what conditions the same rule would operate in other number bases. Problems could then be prepared by pupils for one another.

Teacher role

To give pupils 'space' in which to attack a problem, the role of the teacher shifts. While the pupils are problem solving, the teacher is a resource. The problems and the materials are probably provided by the teacher. From then on, the decisions are taken by the problem solvers and the teacher becomes an observer, occasionally a guide reminding pupils of a helpful question, or a useful procedure, or possibly directing their attention towards a resolution of a different problem which might have some relevance to their current work. There is no marking to be done, since a problem is finally tidied up and presented in a way that is convincing to others. The teacher is ready to ask awkward questions, or to focus on constraints which have been overlooked. Together with the pupils, the teacher helps to decide what form the presentations should take. Will each group present their results to the class, if all are working differently? If all are working on the same problem, will all the results be displayed so that comparisons are made? Will a file of work relating to particular problems be collected, perhaps to be shown on a parents' evening? The whole class can take responsibility for making these kinds of decisions and then it is the teacher's role to ensure that the decision is implemented. This role leaves the teacher free to work alongside particular pupils, building confidence and supporting attempts.

Who is doing the thinking?

The ability of the child does not dictate whether or not she or he can think although it does probably indicate with what complexity and sophistication thinking is carried out. Instead of coding information so that the thinking behind it is more and more removed, problem solving demands that the thinking takes place and passes the responsibility for that thinking back to the pupil. This has a stimulating effect on both the quality of the thinking and on the attitudes of the pupil. Sometimes inert knowledge which was learnt from a text is released into a context which gives it meaning and the pupil is exhilarated at making the connections. As teachers we can do everything for our pupils up to, but not including, making their connections for them. At that point it really is over to them. Problem solving provides them with an opportunity, and the teacher, vicariously, with a share in the resultant excitement.

6 HAVE THE PUPILS GAINED?

There is no simple answer to the question, 'Have the pupils gained from this activity?'. Neither is it reasonable to expect that pupils' mathematical behaviour will immediately change. Learning can follow a slow, sometimes tortuous, route along which small increments may accumulate into a substantial shift. It is often difficult for a teacher to be patient while pupils make that shift in the way, and the time, that best suits them. They may 'help' or 'tell', thereby denying pupils the opportunity to create their own connections. One reason for this is that lessons are seen as being the opportunity to learn something new, or develop a new skill. So, telling or showing becomes a natural part of a teacher's repertoire of behaviour. But every lesson is an amalgam not only of content but also of method, style, personal experience and attitudes. Frequently pupils perceive what is being taught quite differently from the teacher. In looking for pupil gains in these circumstances, the teacher might decide that the lesson was not successful whereas the pupils might have learnt something quite powerful that was unintended. Conversely, a topic may appear to have been 'covered' in a lesson, but the pupils have not in fact retained very much.

The developments that might have taken place in the pupils might not be those most desired or expected. Looking only for gains in knowledge or skills might lead us to look in vain. Perhaps the pupils were learning what it feels like to be in that class, how they see themselves in relation to that subject matter, whether their contribution is valued or not, who 'owns' the knowledge, where that knowledge comes from and whether they can have access to it, and so on. These aspects of learning will affect their next experience so they are powerful agents. Check-lists, therefore, while bringing comfort to teachers or parents who are looking for evidence that time is being well spent, trivialise the complexity of learning and development.

None the less, the teacher is likely to feel uncomfortable if she or he cannot explain what is happening in the class, nor why. The complexity of the mathematics classroom will therefore be examined by looking at four components in turn, remembering that in practice they are intertwined. The four components are personal changes, social changes, process changes and mathematical changes.

Personal changes

'Please, miss, what do I do now?'
'Please, sir, I've finished. What do I do next?'
'May I have the scissors?'
'Where do the crayons go?'

These types of questions, which can frequently be heard in classrooms, are indicative of the dependency which arises. Taken individually, each one might be perfectly reasonable, but together they indicate that the classroom and its resources 'belong' to the teacher. Such dependency not only undermines the authority and confidence that, as teachers, we want to nurture in our pupils, but it has implications for where the responsibility for learning lies. Out of dependency can develop poor self-image, negative attitudes, and boredom. In establishing problem investigations as a regular feature of classroom life, the pupils are being encouraged to take responsibility for their choice of problem, for their collaborators, for their method of attack, for the style of report which they make on completion of their work. Indeed, even the decision about when they have completed the work is theirs to make. Not only does this leave the teacher free to observe pupils' mathematical behaviour and hear statements which can frequently surprise by their insight, but it also profoundly affects the attitudes of the pupils.

The first sign of change is a sense of commitment to what is being done. Instead of hurrying out of class, or abandoning the work at the first chance, pupils continue into their free time, sometimes staying in the classroom when the others go out at break, sometimes working on the problem at home. Teachers have commented on how pupils who are reluctant to do homework will spend a number of hours on a problem, frequently involving other members of the family.

Along with this sense of commitment pupils display a sense of enjoyment. They freely speak of the pleasure their problem solving has given them, often mentioning how 'unlike mathematics' or 'more enjoyable than mathematics' it was. Together with enjoyment goes a new sense of the possible, a re-evaluation of their capacity. Pupils whose attainment in mathematics has been poor often astonish their teachers, and themselves, at what they can accomplish. If pupils are allowed to continue working from one session to another without pressure to complete or abandon, they can work at a pace most suitable to them. Removing such pressures seems to allow space for the use of imagination and creativity which gives the pupil a strong sensation of 'owning' the resulting work.

Michael Armstrong drew attention to this in *Closely Observed Children* (p.90), his sensitive diary of a class of eight-year-olds. He wrote,

Sally came to show me what she had made with the ball bearings, the card and the magnet. Her face was alive with pleasure and a kind of inner excitement. I noticed this particularly, because Sally quite often feigns a mild disdain, almost a world weariness, in relation to herself and her activity in the classroom.

Personal gains will be remarked in terms of independence, enjoyment, personal competence and positive attitudes. Evidence for these will be gathered from observing the pupils and the statements they make, and from a noticeably increased commitment to their activities.

Social changes

Harlen, Darwin and Murphy have described in *Match and Mismatch* (p.27) how,

> Children will sometimes learn more efficiently when working individually rather than with others. We must acknowledge that, in these cases, the help or presence of another will in no way enhance their learning. There are, however, many more instances when the interchange of ideas, discussion and joint effort, play a vital and active part in the child's work.

The opportunity to work together at a problem provides an experience for the pupils which, in many cases, is quite new in the mathematics classroom. They themselves report that the number of ideas always exceeds those that one person would have and that different members of the group can contribute different interpretations or approaches.

Working together also affords pupils the chance to explore meaning in their own terms as they share ideas and investigate outcomes. At the same time, the teacher listens and can appreciate what pupils do and do not understand by the fluency with which they discuss a problem. Convincing a group member of an idea is a good test of how well the pupil understands it herself and frequently the teacher finds that pupil-to-pupil communication is more easily understood than teacher-to-pupil.

Employers might tend to rely upon public assessments, done individually, as mechanisms for entry, but they none the less underline the necessity for collaborative problem-solving skills in many areas of employment. The more work of this kind that the pupils do, the easier it becomes both to organise and to assess. To begin with, teachers are frequently concerned that one child will dominate the group, or the brightest child will do all the work. It is not long before the pupils remove this fear by learning how to handle the dominant child, or learning to evaluate the different skills of different children. A sense of fair play usually ensures that each pupil makes a contribution to the work and the negotiation is invaluable.

Working together influences many aspects of development. If the lesson is not the responsibility of the teacher, then the class as a whole has responsibility, as well as every individual within that class. An individual sense of commitment and enthusiasm can then be translated into a group, and class, pattern of behaviour. Social gains will be measured in terms of fruitful collaboration, acceptance of responsibility, an outcome which has been planned and executed by working together. Pupils who have gained socially will be able to listen to one another, use others' ideas, present an argument convincingly, make contributions to a general plan.

Process changes

Some of the processes which were listed in Chapter 4 only need resuscitation in the classroom and the ability and inventiveness of the pupils will delight and astonish. For example, by encouraging pupils to Introduce a representation (P1.6) whenever they begin trying to solve a problem, one opens the door to using whatever means appear natural to them. Figure 10 is the attempt by two children in a class of 9- to 10-year-olds, of Crossing the River (Problem 23).

CROSSING THE RIVER

First we got cuisenaire cubes
and got out two cubes for the boys
and two cubes for the men.
and made a modle of it all.
We strarted moving the cubes.
about. It looked easy at first
but we soon found it wasen't
so easy. We were moving the cubes about
for some time and then we had got
it into a posestion that we saw
we were all most there. We
saw the answer and moved the
cubes and they were all on the
other side.

Figure 10

Meanwhile, Figure 11 shows how three other children demonstrated their resolution of the same problem:

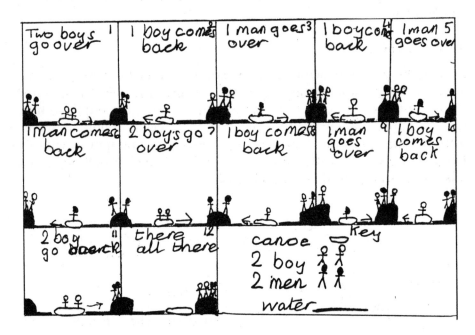

Figure 11

The methods which the pupils use to convince others that their resolution is a good one are many and varied. Frequently, they will 'invent' representational forms which might well form part of their mathematics curriculum at another time. This emphasises again that knowledge acquired in the process of searching for an answer to something one wants to know is more useful than that offered under more formal conditions.

Some procedures need to be mentioned repeatedly so that the pupils acquire the habits which they represent, for example P2.0: Be systematic. In the search for pattern and relationship, system is a necessary condition of success. Pupils need to be reminded of its power both in their own work and when the teacher is demonstrating something systematically. By hiding such problem-solving procedures inside the normal work and assuming that their power will be obvious to the pupils we ensure the opposite. If you want your class to demonstrate systematic approaches, stress this and demonstrate your own systematic approaches when you are working in front of them.

Watch the difference between P1.7: Introduce a form of recording and P2.17: Develop the recording system. In the early stages of tackling the problem, the recording might be crude and informal but sufficient for the job. Only when the problem has been attacked and the pupils are thinking of ways of formalising their work might the necessity arise to develop from informal to more formal means of recording. Pupils should not be inhibited by somewhat messy, informal jottings from proceeding with their problem. As long as they understand what they are doing and they are not yet ready to convince anyone else, there are no grounds for criticising their informality. If they want to explain to the teacher what they have found out and the informal jottings are inadequate to enable this to happen, they will have learnt from their experience why results are presented differently from work in action. By working on different problems and in different groups an excellent reason is provided for pupils to write out their findings so that everyone else can understand. Too often, written work has no rationale for its existence other than classroom demands. This form of work provides its own rationale. Many of the results of the pupils will be arrived at when the teacher is working with another group. Consequently a record to which reference can be made will be important to pupil–teacher communication.

One technique developed in France (see N. Balacheff and M. Guillerant in Bibliography) is very valuable in generating clear and explicit records: pupils who have resolved a problem write a message to their friends to enable them to do likewise. This might require the statement of a generalisation, or it might involve description of a sequence of moves. Pupils usually find this exceedingly difficult to do and it challenges their comprehension and understanding of the problem as well as their verbal, symbolic and diagrammatic abilities. Another good device is to ask pupils who have succeeded to invent a new problem for their friends as a result of what they have found out. This is a use by them of Review-Extension Procedures such as P3.6: Creating different problems. For the teacher, it provides evidence of what the pupils have accomplished as well as ensuring a continuing sequence of activity.

In Problem 8 (Village Streets), an ability to make a clear drawing is all that is required to get started. However, progress will only be made if the pupils can make and test conjectures, and finally articulate a generalisation relating numbers of streets to numbers of crossroads. This is a good opportunity to try the message-writing technique mentioned above by asking the pupils to write a message to tell some friends if they knew how many streets there were, how many street lights would be required. What about the reverse?

Figure 12 demonstrates how good drawing ability did not help Liz,

Kerry and Jeanette, aged 11 years, to get very far with this problem:

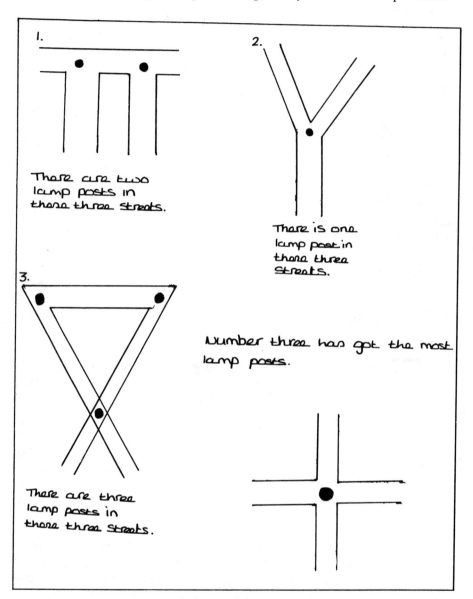

1.

There are two
lamp posts in
those three streets.

2.

There is one
lamp post in
those three
streets.

Number three has got the most
lamp posts.

3.

There are three
lamp posts in
those three streets.

Figure 12

In Figure 13, on the other hand, Billy and Darren, two 12-year-olds, made some progress:

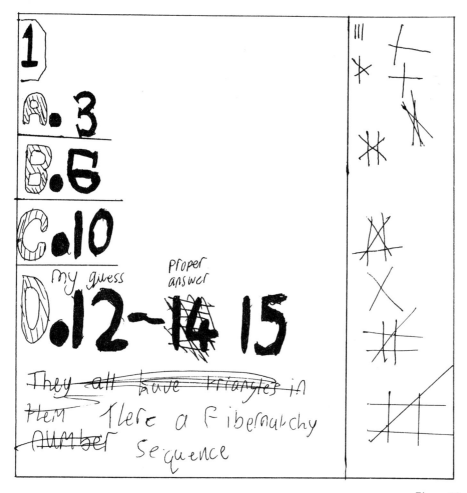

Figure 13

If pupils recognise triangular numbers, then this problem provides a good opportunity for them to use that knowledge. If they do not, and have not met triangular numbers before, they could still make something of the problem but would be less likely to recognise the number pattern. Note how, for Billy and Darren, providing a label, the Fibonacci Sequence, appeared to them to be enough to resolve the problem whereas, in fact, they would not have been able to write a message relating streets to crossroads.

The list of Skills and Procedures offers one way of assessing the processes gained in problem-solving activities. However, it would be foolish to expect that these processes will become a normal part of the pupils' repertoire of behaviours unless time is spent reflecting on their use. The key is to make the processes overt by drawing attention to them when they are useful and recalling their use reflectively when they might be helpful. Each problem is analysed in terms of the appropriate skills and procedures; this aids the teacher in drawing useful skills and procedures to the attention of pupils, and in assessing the use made of them. To make such an analysis of a problem the teacher should work through it, preferably with someone else, and then list the skills and procedures that were appropriate.

Mathematical changes

Most of the problems in this book require very little mathematical knowledge in order to get started. They also do not overtly 'teach' new aspects of mathematics although they might well highlight relationships which the pupils have not previously observed. Thus, in Making Toast (Problem 5) the numbers involved are small and easy to manipulate but the reasoning can take the pupil right through to a generalisation about any number of slices of bread related to the capacity of the grill. Pupils invent very interesting representations for this problem. Figures 14 to 16 show how Jason, Nathan and Juliette, aged 10 years, drew it:

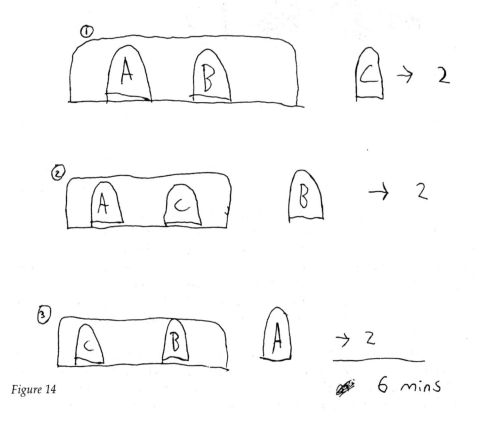

Figure 14

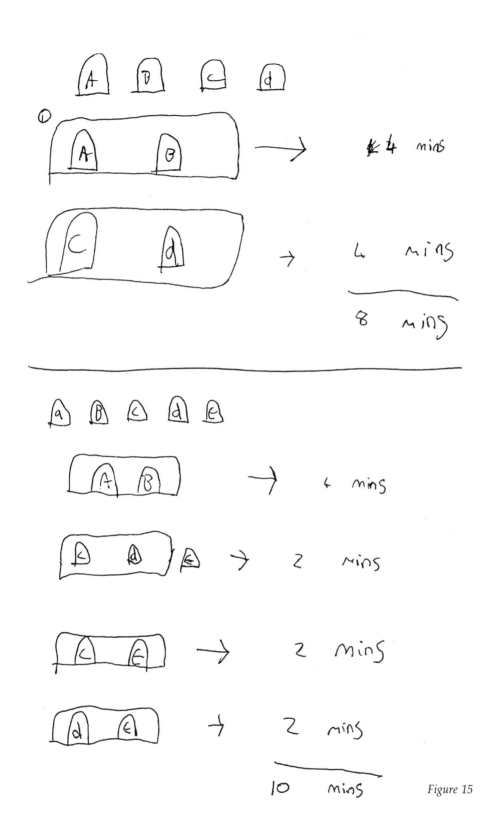

Figure 15

59

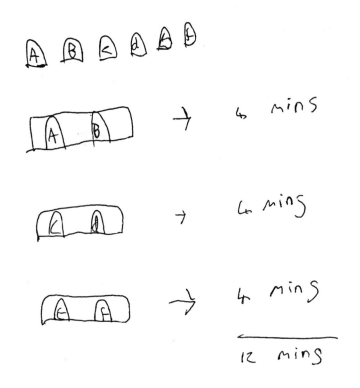

4 mins

6 mins

4 mins

12 mins

we know that is we had ten
slices of toast it would take 20 mins
to roast both sides or each
slice of toast because five
slices of toast take ten mins 20 mins
so ten slices of toast it would take →

Figure 16

Banwell, Saunders and Tahta describe in *Starting Points* how,

It is sometimes said that mathematics is essentially problem solving.
This can be misleading if by this is meant the getting of answers to
problems which are well-defined and understood. At the start of a
mathematical activity a problem is rarely well-defined. Preliminary
mental 'doodling' begins to clarify the outlines and very often the
resolution consists of a re-definition or a refinement of the problem so
that it fits into the scheme developed during the doodling. This fitting
and refitting is rarely mentioned in mathematical literature today,
though some of the great classic papers are full of subjective accounts
of the mental paths which led to the final result. The importance of
mathematics in education lies in process rather than product. An
actual formula for the number of squares the diagonal of a rectangle

60

passes through is not, after all, an important thing to possess. The process of getting a formula is.

So have the pupils gained? If they are using their mathematical thinking, skills and knowledge, working together, and, in the process, feeling confident and competent; if they are enthusiastic and showing evident signs of enjoyment you will know that they have gained and as their teacher, you too will have gained.

7 PROBLEMS 1–30

TYPE OF PROBLEM (see p.19)

Description of the problem as presented to the pupil

SOLVER SHOULD KNOW

- mathematical knowledge or skills essential to the resolution. This helps classroom organisation as problems outside the competencies of pupils can be withheld or deliberately used to back up other lessons.

  A blank for this section indicates that the problem can be attempted without prior knowledge.

MATERIALS TO USE

- useful materials for setting up the problem are listed where relevant

FOR THE TEACHER

Suggests ways in which pupils can be helped without closing the problem or making the resolution teacher-dominated.

The Organising Questions, Procedures and Skills which are appropriate to each problem are listed here. Those printed in bold are particularly relevant to that problem.

RESOLUTION AND NOTES

A range of possible resolutions is given for each problem.

EXTENSIONS

Some extensions to the problem are given together with a guide to their use.

Mathematical Note
In some cases mathematical notes are provided for teachers who are interested but these can be ignored without affecting the implementation of the problem.

1   RABBITS AND HUTCHES

There are some rabbits and some rabbit hutches. If seven rabbits are put in each rabbit hutch, one rabbit is left over. If nine rabbits are put in each rabbit hutch, one hutch is left empty.

Can you find how many rabbit hutches and how many rabbits there are?

SOLVER SHOULD KNOW

- elementary number work (subtraction, division by 2)

MATERIALS TO USE

- if pupils want to use a concrete representation for the rabbits and hutches, use something plentiful like counters

FOR THE TEACHER

Make sure the children are aware of the information given in the problem. Suggest trying pairs of numbers of rabbits and hutches systematically. Encourage children to record their attempts.

Help the children make connections, for example between the number of hutches and the way in which the rabbits are distributed.

Organising Questions **1.1, 2.1,**
  (p.28)
Procedures 1.2, 1.6, 1.7, 2.0, 2.4, 2.6,
  2.11, 3.6 (pp.3–4)

Skills 1.1, 2.1 (p.41)

RESOLUTION AND NOTES

There are 36 rabbits and five hutches. Children are not expected to know or use algebra; systematic trial and error will give the answer.

Picking numbers randomly and trying them is perhaps necessary in the Entry stage but for Attack, children should be encouraged to work systematically, with a plan, and to record their attempts.

Trying numbers of hutches systematically and seeing how many rabbits each piece of information gives is a good way:

h	number of hutches	1	2	3	4	5	6	7
r	rabbits, from $7h+1$	8	15	22	29	36	43	50
r	rabbits, from $9(h-1)$	0	9	18	27	36	45	54

Mathematical Note
Let h = number of hutches and r = number of rabbits.
Then $r = 7h+1$ and $r = 9 (h-1)$.
Therefore $7h+1 = 9h-9$,
so $2h = 10$, $h = 5$ and $r = 36$.

EXTENSIONS

1 The numbers 7 and 9 can be changed, but not arbitrarily. The difference between the two numbers has to be a factor of the larger plus one (here $(9-7)$ is a factor of $(9+1)$).

2 Children may find it interesting to invent similar problems by working backwards, e.g. assume there are 40 rabbits.
Since $40 = 3 \times 13 + 1$
$\quad\quad\quad = (3-1) \times 20,$
we could have a rabbit problem with 13 rabbits in each hutch initially, then 20 rabbits.

2 FACTORS

number	factors
1	1
2	1 2
3	1 • 3
4	1 2 • 4
5	1 • • • 5
6	1 2 3 • • 6

This table shows the numbers from 1 to 6 with their factors. The number 4, for example, has factors 1, 2 and 4, with no number in the space for 3.

Make your own table for the numbers up to 30. See what you can find out about numbers with only two factors. Can you guess the next one? What sort of numbers are they?

Now try three factors and then four factors. See if you can guess the next number with three factors and then with four, and explain why. What sort of numbers have an odd number of factors? Can you find other patterns in your table?

SOLVER SHOULD KNOW

- how to find factors
- how to use a calculator
- prime, square and rectangular numbers

MATERIALS TO USE

- squared paper for systematic presentation
- a calculator

FOR THE TEACHER

Direct the pupils' attention to the number patterns, e.g. square numbers. The patterns can be investigated by checking the table to verify predicted numbers. It is crucial that the numbers are arranged systematically if a pattern is to be observed.

Pupils will find it easier to complete a line of factors horizontally *and* vertically if they realise how and why the pattern works (e.g. a number occurring as a factor of every third number).

Organising Questions **2.3, 2.4** (p.29)
Procedures 1.3, 1.5, 1.7, 2.0, 2.1, 2.2,
  2.7, 2.19, 3.6 (pp.31–40)

Skills 1.1, 1.2, 1.3, 3.1, 3.2, 4.1, 4.2, 5.2
  (pp.41–44)

RESOLUTION AND NOTES

Number of factors		Pattern
1		1 is a special case
2	2,3,5,7,11,13,17,19,23,29	prime numbers
3	4,9,25	prime numbers squared
4	6,8,10,14,15,21,22,26,27	rectangular numbers
5	16	fourth powers of prime numbers
6	12,18,20,27	rectangular numbers: 2 rectangles
7	none under 64	sixth powers of prime numbers
8	30	rectangular numbers: 3 rectangles

In general:
Numbers with an odd number of factors
are square numbers.
Numbers with two factors are prime, the
factors are 1 and the number itself.
Numbers with four, six, eight . . . factors
are rectangular. Four factors means only
one rectangle may be drawn: 6 as 2×3;
6 factors means two rectangles may be
drawn: 12 as 2×6 or 3×4.

Mathematical Note
A number of form $p^m.q^n$ has $(m+1)(n+1)$
factors if p and q are prime. Because
$(m+1)(n+1)$ is only odd if m and n are
both even, only perfect squares have an
odd number of factors.
  More generally a number of form
$p_1^{a_1} p_2^{a_2} \ldots . p_n^{a_n}$ (where p_1 is prime) has
$(a_1+1)(a_2+1) \ldots . (a_n+1)$ factors.

EXTENSIONS

1 There are many patterns in the table,
e.g. the checking pattern. Diagonal lines
will give the times tables.

2 Find a number with seven factors (64 is
one). Find a number with nine factors (36
is one).

3 Investigate the product of all the
factors of a number. It is related to the
number of factors.

3   THE MILK CRATE

A milk crate holds 24 bottles and is shaped like this:

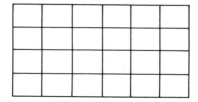

The crate has four rows and six columns. Can you put 18 bottles of milk in the crate so that each row and each column of the crate has an *even* number of bottles in it? Is there only one way to do it?

SOLVER SHOULD KNOW

MATERIALS TO USE

- a geoboard or squared paper
- 18 counters

FOR THE TEACHER

Encourage the pupils to think of things they might need to get started. Concrete representation is more helpful than drawing pictures. Suggest that trials, solutions and pooled results are recorded in some form. Making a systematic search may involve moving one bottle at a time horizontally or vertically, then looking at the effect on rows and columns.

If pupils have difficulties, suggest they change the way they view the problem, for example looking at the arrangement of the six spaces rather than the 18 bottles.

Extend the resolution of the problem by comparing different resolutions or changing the number of bottles or size of crate.

Organising Questions **1.3, 2.6**
  (pp.28–29)
Procedures 1.2, 1.4, 1.6, **1.7**, 2.4, 2.5,

2.7, 2.13, 2.15, **2.17**, 2.18, **3.3**, 3.6
(pp.30–40)
Skills 1.1, 1.3, 2.1 (pp.41–42)

RESOLUTION AND NOTES

The arrangement below is not the only one, but all others are variations on it.

spaces

6	0	0	0	2	2	2	
0	B	B	B	B	B	B	
2	B	B	B			B	bottles
2	B	B	B	B			
·2	B	B	B		B		
	4	4	4	2	2	2	18

There must be one row of 6 bottles and three rows of 4 bottles. There must be three columns of 4 bottles and three columns of 2 bottles.

It is easier to work with six spaces rather than 18 bottles but then zero must be regarded as an even number.
P2.13: Eliminate paths is involved in the resolution of the problem.

Pupils have a tendency to read the word 'even' as 'the same'. The problem then becomes impossible.

If pencil and paper only are used, crossing out or rubbing out to make changes often results in the number of bottles in place not being 18. Counters or small pieces of paper will prevent this.

EXTENSIONS

1 Children have found up to 72 solutions and there are more. Compiling sets of solutions leads to the development of systems for classifying them.

2 When are two solutions 'really the same'?

3 Change the number of milk bottles from 18 to something else. (The problem

is impossible with an odd number of bottles. Is it possible with *any* even number of bottles?)

4 Change the dimension of the milkcrate.

5 Investigate arrangements where there is an even number of bottles in each row and column.

4 CROSSING THE DESERT

A man has to deliver a message across a desert. Crossing the desert takes nine days. One man can only carry enough food to last him 12 days. No food is available where the message must be delivered. Two men set out.

Can the message be delivered and both men return to where they started without going short of food? (Food may be buried on the way out and used on the way back.)

SOLVER SHOULD KNOW

MATERIALS TO USE

- squared paper (marked one square per day)
- 12 counters (for food)

FOR THE TEACHER

Make sure pupils concentrate on the information given in the problem and that they have absorbed the four points listed in the 'Resolution' opposite. Ask them to calculate how much food the second man can bury after he has walked for one day, two days and so on.

Squared paper and counters can be used to make a diagram to show the amount of food for each day. A counter is discarded for each day and the buried food left on the appropriate square.

Ask the pupils to consider the problem of how people climb Mt Everest.

Organising Questions **1.1, 2.2** (p.28)
Procedures 1.1, 1.3, 1.4, 1.6, 1.7, 2.1,
2.2, 2.5, 2.6, 2.7, 2.12, 2.13, 2.16, 3.5,
3.6 (pp.30–40)

Skills 1.1, **1.3, 1.4**, 2.1, 2.2, 5.3
(pp.41–44)

RESOLUTION AND NOTES

To resolve the problem it must be realised that:
a) Both men cannot go all the way across and get back without starving.
b) Only one man is needed to carry a message.
c) Both men set out together and at some point one turns back having topped up the food supply of the other to the full allowable 12 days supply.
d) The buried food is picked up by the actual message carrier.

2 men: Both go three days then one turns back. Food analysis: start 24 days, use six to get to the splitting point, messenger takes 12, three buried, three for the other man to get home.

3 men: All go four days then two turn back. Food analysis: start 36 days, use 12 to get to the splitting point, messenger takes 12, four buried, eight for other men to get home.

The hidden condition here is that each man makes only one trip: if portering is allowed, two men can conquer a 10-day desert (split after four days, one man makes a second trip to supply messenger on return leg). This version of the problem is much more complex, especially for larger numbers of men.
If time is allowed to build up stock piles before delivering the message, deserts of any size can be crossed.

EXTENSIONS

1 Children could change the numbers involved (i.e. the nine and the 12) and see if delivering the message is still possible with two men.

2 Is there any advantage in using more than two men in a desert of this size?

3 How much wider could the desert be if three men (four men, five men etc) were available to help deliver the message?

5 MAKING TOAST

There is room in a grill to toast one side of two slices of bread in two minutes. How long does it take to toast both sides of three slices of bread? Is that the quickest way?

Work out the quickest way to toast four slices of bread on both sides. Then try five slices of bread and then six. Can you predict the quickest time for any number of slices? How would you do it? Try again with a grill that holds three or more slices of bread.

SOLVER SHOULD KNOW

MATERIALS TO USE

- young children may want concrete representations for slices of bread which can be marked when they have been 'toasted', e.g. paper, Plasticine

FOR THE TEACHER

Ask children to look for a pattern so that attention is drawn to the time taken for different numbers of slices.

Use a notation or pictorial representation to record how the grilling has been done. Remember that a half-done slice can have its second side grilled later so that you avoid using the grill twice to toast one side of one piece of bread.

Change the way the problem is tackled by dealing with both sides of one slice consecutively.

Make a generalisation for the quickest time and method used.

Organising Questions **2.3** (p.29)
Procedures 1.4, 1.6, 1.7, 2.1, 2.2, 2.7,
  2.14, **2.16,** 2.17, **2.19** (pp.31–39)

Skills 1.1, 1.3, 2.1, 2.2, 2.3, 4.1, 4.2, 5.2
  (pp.41–44)

RESOLUTION AND NOTES

The notation used here is as follows: each slice is lettered in order of insertion, A, B and so on. The following number gives the side, e.g. B2 is the second side of the second slice.

2-slice grill
3 slices: A1 B1, A2 C1, B2 C2 6 minutes.
4, 6, 8, 10 . . . slices are all multiples of 2, so the grill is always full anyway.
5 slices: first two slices as usual then follow pattern above.
(same for 7, 9, 11 slices)

3-slice grill
3, 6, 9 . . . slices are all multiples of 3, so the grill is always full anyway.
4 slices: A1 B1 C1, A2 B2 D1, – C2 D2.
5 slices: A1 B1 C1, A2 B2 D1,
C2 E1 D2, – E2 –.
(same for 8, 11, 14 slices)

To calculate the minimum number of times you need to use the grill, multiply the number of slices by 2, divide by the capacity of the grill and round up to the nearest whole number.

EXTENSIONS

1 Encourage children to consider grills of different sizes. Some may discover the rule given at the end of the resolution.

2 Change the problem by specifying the time taken to turn a slice over and take a slice out or put it in.

6 MAKING TRIANGLES

Using 12 rods of varying lengths how many different triangles can you make?

What *types* of triangle can you make? Can you make a triangle with *any* three rods? What about 2, 3 and 5 or 2, 2 and 3?

SOLVER SHOULD KNOW

- different types of triangle, e.g. equilateral, isosceles, scalene, right-angled, obtuse-angled (not all are essential)

MATERIALS TO USE

- three rods 2-units long, three rods 3-units long, three rods 4-units long, three rods 5-units long
- the children can make their own rods from paper sticks or straws (Centicubes or Cuisenaire rods are too thick)

FOR THE TEACHER

Encourage pupils to break down the problem, perhaps by holding all the variables constant except one, e.g. try equilateral triangles first then vary the length of one side at a time.

Organising Questions **2.5** (p.29)
Procedures 1.3, 1.4, **2.0**, 2.1, 2.2, 2.3,
2.5, **2.9**, 2.16, 2.17, 3.6 (pp.31–40)

Skills 1.2, 1.4, 2.1, 2.2, 3.1 (pp.41–43)

RESOLUTION AND NOTES

The following triangles are possible:

Triangle			E	I	R	S
2	2	2	×			
2	2	3		×		
*						
*						
2	3	3		×		
2	3	4				×
*						
2	4	4		×		
2	4	5				×
2	5	5		×		
3	3	3	×			
3	3	4		×		
3	3	5		×		
3	4	4		×		
3	4	5			×	×
3	5	5		×		
4	4	4	×			
4	4	5		×		
4	5	5		×		
5	5	5	×			

E equilateral
I isosceles
R right-angled
S scalene (all sides different)

* certain combinations do not give a triangle: 2, 2, 4; 2, 2, 5; and 2, 3, 5

Triangles can also be classified according to the size of the largest angle, i.e. obtuse-angled or not.

Some form of systematic control of variables (P2.9) is needed to find all of the possible triangles. The list given here is a typical example of the result of totally systematic control of variables and ensures completeness.

EXTENSIONS

1 Change the set of rods being used.

2 Make quadrilaterals using four rods. An extra rod of each length will be required.

3 Encourage children to investigate the question 'How can I tell, without trying it, if three rods will make a triangle?'. (Each one must be shorter than the total length of the other two.)

7 NO TRIANGLES ALLOWED

Draw four dots on a circle and join each dot to the next dot with a straight line. Can you draw any more straight lines, joining up the dots *without* making any triangles?

Try the same thing for five dots, six dots, seven dots and so on, getting in as many lines as you can. Can you fill in a table of the number of dots and number of lines? Predict how many lines can be drawn without making triangles when there are 13 dots. What sort of number never appears in the second column of the table?

SOLVER SHOULD KNOW

- number patterns
- general drawing ability

MATERIALS TO USE

- pencil, paper, ruler
- compasses are not essential as circles can be drawn round a coin or drawn freehand
- a circular geoboard is useful if available

FOR THE TEACHER

Draw pupils' attention to the most basic aspect of the question, i.e. focus on the four-dot case. The dots can be anywhere on the circle but should be well spaced. Six dots is the smallest number requiring extra lines across the circle.

See if there is a pattern. If the table is completed systematically the absence of '3' under 'number of lines' will be evident.

Organising Questions **1.2, 2.3**
  (pp.28–29)
Procedures 1.3, 1.4, 1.7, **2.0**, 2.1, 2.2,
  2.7, 2.10, 2.13, 2.19, 3.5 (pp.31–40)

Skills 1.1, 1.2, 1.3, 3.1, 4.1, 4.2, 5.3
  (pp.41–44)

RESOLUTION AND NOTES

The full table includes the cases for 1, 2 and 3 dots which are not asked for in the problem.

number of dots	1	2	3	4	5	6	7	8	9	10	11	12
number of lines	0	1	2	4	5	7	8	10	11	13	14	16

Multiples of 3 never appear in the second column of the table: 3 does not appear because with three dots you can only draw two lines without making a triangle on the circle. 6 does not appear because with six dots you can draw in a diagonal, to make seven lines.

Adding a seventh dot means only one more line, no extra diagonals can be drawn.
  With eight dots a second diagonal can be added, 10 lines not nine.
  The pattern is that for every two new dots after 6, an extra diagonal can be drawn.

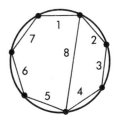

7 dots

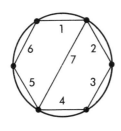

6 dots

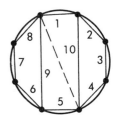

8 dots

EXTENSIONS

1 Not making *quadrilaterals* or some other specified shape might be interesting.

2 Allowing triangles like (a) but not like (b).

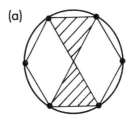

(a)

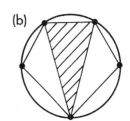

(b)

8 VILLAGE STREETS

> In a village there are three streets. All the streets are straight. One lamp-post is put up at each crossroads.
>
> What is the greatest number of lamp-posts that could be needed? Now try four streets and five streets. Predict the answer for six streets then check it. Can you see a pattern? Why does the pattern work?

SOLVER SHOULD KNOW

- drawing ability (the lines must be long enough to enable new lines to cut them and every pair of lines must meet on the page)

MATERIALS TO USE

- long thin straws are good for representing streets

FOR THE TEACHER

Help the children to get started by encouraging the use of representations. Suggest they look for a pattern by drawing up a table connecting the number of streets with the number of lamp-posts.

Make them aware of how and why the pattern works by seeing what happens to the number of intersections with existing streets, each time a new street is added.

Vary the problem by allowing streets to cross at any angle.

STRATEGIES AND SKILLS

Organising Questions **1.3, 2.3, 2.4** (pp.28–29)

Procedures 1.1, 1.3, 1.6, **2.1, 2.2, 2.3, 2.4, 2.7**, 2.10, **2.16**, 2.17, 2.18, 2.19, 3.6 (pp.30–40)

Skills 1.1, 1.3, 2.1, 2.2, 2.3, 3.2, 4.1, 4.2, 5.2, 5.3 (pp.41–44)

There is a tendency to draw the streets parallel to, or at right angles to, each other. This 'set' does not give the greatest number of crossroads (P2.16). Each new street added can be drawn to cross all the existing streets. Exploring (P1.1) or playing with the problem is usually involved in the Entry process. The number pattern involved is that of the triangular numbers.

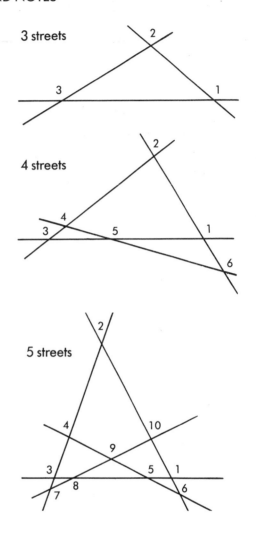

3 streets

4 streets

5 streets

number of streets	number of posts
1	0
2	1
3	3
4	6
5	10
6	15

Encourage the children to use the arrangement for four streets to build up the arrangement for five streets and so on.

Labelling the streets A, B, C, D etc and the intersections AB, AC, AD, BC etc will enable some children to find later results without complicated diagrams.

EXTENSIONS

1 What if the streets are either parallel or perpendicular?

2 Triangular numbers occur in quite a number of contexts and problems.

See for example Problem 30 and Extensions for Problems 12 and 13.

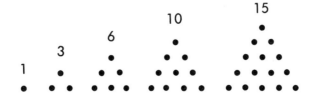

9 AFTERNOON TEA PARTY

Some people had afternoon tea in a cafe which only sold tea and cakes. Tea cost 3p a cup, cakes cost 5p each. Everyone had the same number of cakes and the same number of cups of tea. The bill came to £1.33.

Can you find out how many cups of tea each person had?

SOLVER SHOULD KNOW

- multiplication, division and addition of integers

MATERIALS TO USE

- paper and pencil
- a calculator can be an advantage (money seems to hinder as often as it helps)

FOR THE TEACHER

Suggest pupils look at connections between the number of people and the bill for each person. Encourage them to make and test guesses. This helps establish that 133 must be factored into the number of people and the bill.

They can test different factors by trying particular cases such as the bill for two people.

If a child cannot make progress, suggest a related problem, e.g. a bill of 39p.

Organising Questions **2.1, 2.2** (pp.28–29)

Procedures **1.1, 1.2,** 1.3, 1.4, 1.6, 1.7, 2.0, **2.1, 2.2,** 2.4, **2.5,** 2.6, **2.8,** 2.9, 2.16, 3.4, 3.5, 3.6 (pp.30–40)

Skills 1.1, 1.2, 1.3, 2.1, 2.2, 3.1 (pp.41–43)

RESOLUTION AND NOTES

The bill for each person must be a divisor of 133, so must be 1, 7, 19 or 133. The bill cannot be 1p or 7p each, because 5p and 3p are the only prices. The bill cannot be 133p for each person because we assume there is more than one person.

Since $19 = (2 \times 5) + (3 \times 3)$, the answer is three cups of tea each.

Children should try combinations of tea and cakes and try dividing 133 by the total cost of each combination.

Systematic trials should be encouraged, e.g.:

number of people	each person's bill	is this possible?
1	133p	no
2	66½p	no – why?
3	44½p	no – why?
.	.	.
.	.	.

P1.2: Make and test guesses is a useful Entry procedure here. P2.5: Try particular cases, used systematically, can be used to attack the problem.

Specific questions such as 'If there were two people, how much would each have to pay?' will be needed to get children started on the preliminary trials.

EXTENSIONS

The prices and the total bill can be changed. Often there will be more than one solution.

10 PERFECT NUMBERS

What numbers go into 6 exactly? 6, 3, 2 and 1 do. Do you notice that
$6 = 3 + 2 + 1$? 6 is called a *perfect* number because it is equal to the
sum of the other numbers which go into it exactly.
What is the next perfect number?

SOLVER SHOULD KNOW

- division, multiplication tables up to 10
- factors
- data obtained in Problem 2

MATERIALS TO USE

- pencil and paper
- calculator

FOR THE TEACHER

Encourage the children to use the
information given in the problem. They
could try some other numbers; small
ones are best to start with. Make sure the
children understand what a perfect
number is.

Suggest that they try numbers
systematically and record results. Don't
suggest children find the third perfect
number (496) without help. Ask them to
check that 496 is indeed perfect – this
may lead to interesting patterns.

RESOLUTION AND NOTES

The concrete operational method is to try out and tabulate systematically. The formal operational method is to eliminate many possible numbers in a more general manner. A prime number can be eliminated because there is only one other number (1) that goes into it.

The first six perfect numbers are:

$$6$$
$$28$$
$$496$$
$$8\,128$$
$$33\,550\,336$$
$$8\,589\,869\,056.$$

Only 17 perfect numbers are known.

Hints are required if the children wish to find the third perfect number, but checking that 496 and 8 128 are perfect can be profitable.

P1.3: Define terms and relationships, is a step in the Entry procedure. The meaning of the term 'perfect number' must be clarified before attacking the problem.

Mathematical Note
All known perfect numbers are differences of certain powers of 2, e.g.
$6 = 2^3 - 2^1$ $28 = 2^5 - 2^2$
$496 = 2^8 - 2^4$

EXTENSIONS

Other properties of a number can make interesting problems. Numbers can be divided into *perfect, abundant* and *deficient*. Abundant numbers are less than the sum of their divisors (other than the number itself) and deficient numbers are more than this sum, e.g. 24 has divisors:

1, 2, 3, 4, 5, 6, 8, 12, 24. Because $1 + 2 + 3 + 4 + 6 + 8 + 12 = 36$, 24 is an abundant number.

22 is deficient because $22 > 1 + 2 + 11$.

Classify numbers in this way – can you see any patterns?

11 CHANGING FIFTY PENCE

The other day I was asked if I could change a 50 pence piece. I had more than 50 pence in coins in my pocket but I could not make exactly 50 pence.

Can you find several ways this could happen? What is the largest amount I could have had in my pocket?

SOLVER SHOULD KNOW

MATERIALS TO USE

- play money (the total amount should be greater than the amount needed)

FOR THE TEACHER

Encourage the children to find results that help towards the solution, perhaps by using the related problem of changing 10 pence. Encourage the children to develop a form of recording.

Help the children to avoid the attitude that 'of course you can change 50 pence if you have coins worth more'.

Organising Questions **2.2, 2.6** (p.29)
Procedures 1.1, 1.2, 1.3, 1.6, **1.7**, 2.0,
2.1, 2.4, 2.5, **2.8**, 2.9, 2.10, 2.13, **2.16**,
3.4 (pp.30–40)

Skills **1.3**, 1.4, 3.1 (pp.41–43)

━━━━━━━━━━ RESOLUTION AND NOTES ━━━━━━━━━━

The reason change cannot be given is that the coins in the pocket will only make odd amounts around 50p. The table below gives an idea of the possibilities:

The largest amount is therefore 53½p.
    Note that all or some of the 10p pieces can be swopped for 5p pieces, giving many more possible answers.

10p	5p	2p	½p	Total
4	1	3	–	51p
4	1	3	1	51½p
4	1	4	–	53p
4	1	4	1	53½p

━━━━━━━━━━ EXTENSIONS ━━━━━━━━━━

Change for £1, £5 are possibilities. The results here can use the previous results obtained.

12 BADMINTON GAME

Janet, Sangita, Anne and Margaret like to play badminton together but cannot all be free to play on the same day. Janet is unable to play on Tuesdays, Wednesdays and Saturdays. Sangita is free to play on Mondays, Wednesdays and Thursdays. Anne has to stay at home on Mondays and Thursdays. Margaret can play on Mondays, Tuesdays and Fridays. None of them play on Sundays.

Can each pair find a day on which to play? Are there any days when no games can be played? Are there any days when more than one game can be played?

SOLVER SHOULD KNOW

- experience in sorting out information
- idea of table to record information

MATERIALS TO USE

FOR THE TEACHER

Draw pupils' attention to the information given in the problem, particularly to both negative *and* positive statements. Make sure that they include all the pairs.

Help pupils to get started by encouraging systematic recording, perhaps in tabular form (see opposite).

Organising Questions **1.1, 1.3** (p.28)
Procedures 1.4, 1.5, 1.6, 1.7, 2.0, 2.13, 2.17, 3.5 (pp.31–40)

Skills 1.1, 1.3, 1.4, **2.1, 2.2, 2.3,** 3.1 (pp.41–43)

RESOLUTION AND NOTES

The technique of constructing a table is known as a matrix arrangement and is essential in this type of problem. The problem must be read carefully to distinguish between negative and positive statements; the table must show when people *can* play even if the sentence given says when they *cannot* play.

Each pair can find a day to play.
S1.4: Sorting and categorising information is helpful during the Entry process. This problem demonstrates translation from the linguistic representation of the problem to the pictorial representation of the table.

	Mon	Tue	Wed	Thur	Fri	Sat	Sun
Janet	✓	✗	✗	✓	✓	✗	✗
Sangita	✓	✗	✓	✓	✗	✗	✗
Anne	✗	✓	✓	✗	✓	✓	✗
Margaret	✓	✓	✗	✗	✓	✗	✗

EXTENSIONS

1 What if they can only get one court on any day?

2 How many games can they fit into a week?

3 A different problem is to count the number of games needed when there are 2, 3, 4 . . . people who all want to play. The result is the triangular numbers – see Problem 8.

13 TWO TOWERS

A child has a set of 10 cubes. One cube has 1cm edges, one cube has 2cm edges, one cube has 3cm edges and so on until the largest cube which has 10cm edges.

Can she build two towers of the same height using all the cubes? Show how, or explain why, it can't be done. What difference does it make if another cube with 11cm edges is used as well? Show how to do it in as many ways as possible.

SOLVER SHOULD KNOW

- numbers to 100
- addition
- odd and even numbers

MATERIALS TO USE

- Cuisenaire rods, Unifix, strips of paper or cubes can be used as models
- squared paper can be helpful
- pencil and paper may suffice for older children

FOR THE TEACHER

Help the children to get started by providing materials to model the situation. If a child is stuck, suggest trying, say, six cubes first.

Encourage the children to find results that may help towards the solution. For example, focus on what needs to be used to work out how high each tower will be.

Extend the resolution by adding more cubes or changing the distribution of cube.

Organising Questions **1.3, 2.2, 3.3**
  (pp.28–30)
Procedures 1.1, 1.2, 1.7, 2.0, 2.4, 2.5,
  2.6, 2.10, 2.13, 2.18, 3.4, 3.5 (pp.30–40)

Skills 2.1, 2.2, 2.3, 5.3 (pp.42–44)

RESOLUTION AND NOTES

The problem can be made more concrete by providing models to manipulate. Modelling is involved because a set of cubes will probably not be available and a strip of paper or collections of smaller cubes can be used to model lengths involved.

The first part is impossible: the total height of the cubes is 55cm and two towers of the same height would have to be 27½cm tall.

With the 11cm cube added the new total is 66cm and two 33cm towers can in fact be made as follows:

1
2
5
6
9
10

33

3
4
7
8
11

33

The problem can be turned into one involving numbers rather than cubes or strips of paper representing cubes.

Many other towers can be made by applying P2.10: Use one solution to find others, e.g. the 8cm cube can be interchanged with the 2cm cube and 6cm cube.

EXTENSIONS

1 Change the sets of cubes involved. Triangular numbers are involved in the heights of the towers. The numbers for which the towers can be made make an interesting pattern.

2 How many different solutions can you find to the problem with 11 cubes?

3 Investigate building three towers.

14   A RECTANGLE

The perimeter of a rectangle is 28cm. The length is 10cm more than the width.

What is its length? What is its area? What if the difference were 8cm?

SOLVER SHOULD KNOW

- perimeter, rectangle, area of rectangle

MATERIALS TO USE

- pencil and squared paper

FOR THE TEACHER

Make sure the children read the problem carefully to extract the information given. Encourage them to make connections between length and breadth and the fixed perimeter. Suggest they try some pairs of numbers for the length and width. Draw their attention to these numbers and the relationship between them. The next pair of numbers should be chosen as a result of what has been found from the previous pair.

Organising Questions **1.1, 2.1** (p.28)   Skills 1.1 (p.41)
Procedures 1.2, **1.3**, 1.4, 2.1, 2.2, 2.5, **2.6**
    (pp.30–34)

RESOLUTION AND NOTES

The 'set' is to read the problem as 'the length is 10cm'. The rectangle is 12cm by 2cm. The area is 24cm^2.

There are several ways of attacking the problem: trial and error will work, using number pairs with a difference of 10. This method is better if it is done systematically, with records kept and a plan to choose the next trial in response to the results of the previous trial (P2.6: Adjust guesses).

$(28-20) \div 4$ will give the width. ($2x + 10 = 14$ or $4x + 20 = 28$ are the algebraic forms but children are not expected to use them.)

If the difference is 8cm, the length is 11cm and the area is 33cm^2.

During the Entry phase an important procedure is P1.3: Define terms and relationships. The problem has to be examined in order to find out what the terms mean and what the relationships in the problem are.

EXTENSIONS

Many similar problems can be constructed by working backwards.

Children may like to construct them themselves to give to their friends.

15 PACKING BOXES

Place some boxes with bases 8cm by 6cm on a tray 50cm by 35cm.

If all the boxes have to be placed the same way round, what is the greatest number of boxes which can be placed on the tray? Does it make any difference if the boxes don't all have to be placed on it the same way? What is the greatest number of boxes which can be placed on the tray?

SOLVER SHOULD KNOW

- tiling, tessellation and calculation of area are helpful but not essential
- linear programming can be used

MATERIALS TO USE

- squared paper
- scissors

FOR THE TEACHER

Direct pupils' attention to helpful results that may arise from trying any arrangement of the boxes. Encourage the recording of these attempts.

Area calculations do not provide a reasonable response but give upper limits. Why is this?

Organising Questions **2.2** (p.29)
Procedures 1.1, 1.3, 1.6, 2.0, 2.4, 2.5,
  2.6, 2.14, 2.16, 2.18, 3.5 (pp.30–40)

Skills 1.1, 1.2, 1.4, 2.1, 2.2, 2.3, 3.1
  (pp.30–39)

RESOLUTION AND NOTES

The problem can be made concrete by making model boxes and tray from squared paper and manipulating the arrangement. One resolution is shown to scale below. Spaces round the edges cannot be filled. Consideration of area does not give the real answer which is 35 boxes.

50 cm

6 cm							35
1	2	3	4	5	6	7	
8 cm							34
8	9	10	11	12	13	14	33
15	18	21	24	27		29	32
16	19	22	25	28	30	31	
17	20	23	26				

35 cm

EXTENSIONS

Tiling problems can be interesting. In this case, 'How much bigger must the tray be to enable more boxes to be placed on it?' is another possible problem.

93

16   PUT THE LID ON

Make a large copy of this shape. Cut it out and fold it up; it will make a box.

Where could you add another square onto the shape so that when you cut it out and fold it up you will get a box with a lid?

Find as many shapes as you can which will fold into a box with a lid.

SOLVER SHOULD KNOW

• systematic approach

MATERIALS TO USE

• square paper, scissors
• Sellotape is better than glue

FOR THE TEACHER

Folding is easier with larger squares.
Direct pupils' attention to symmetries as this reduces the number of nets of a cube to be examined.

Procedures 1.1, 2.0, 2.3, 2.10, 2.11, **2.13**,   Skills 3.1, 3.2 (p.43)
   3.6 (pp.30–40)

━━━━━━━━ RESOLUTION AND NOTES ━━━━━━━━

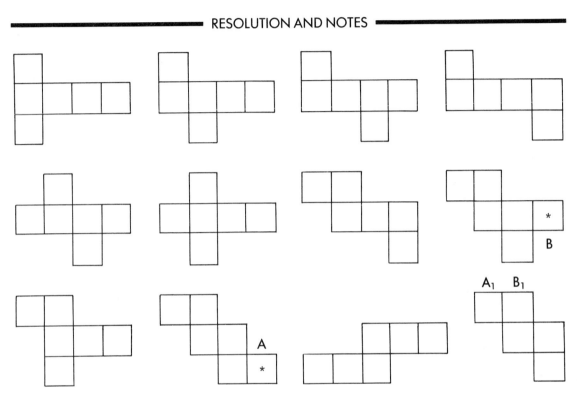

The two nets for cubes marked with a star (*) are the ones which can be made. Putting squares at A_1 or B_1 gives reflections of A and B. All 11 nets for a cube are shown. The wording of the last parts is deliberately open. If children wish to make nets for cuboids they can do so. Finding all the nets for a cube is difficult and children are not expected to find them all, but they can make a good start. Discuss with them which nets are actually the same.

━━━━━━━━ EXTENSIONS ━━━━━━━━

If you wish to pursue the theme of nets *Mathematical Models* by Cundy and Rollett is very useful for this.

17 MARY'S MUDDLE

Mary had two pieces of squared paper, 16 by 8 squares and two pieces 8 by 6 squares.

a) How many more pieces does she need to make a box? What size will the pieces be? What size will the box be?

b) Now begin with two pieces of squared paper 4 by 8 squares, one piece of paper 6 by 8 squares and one piece 4 by 6 squares. What else will you need to make a box?

c) If you have one piece of paper 5 by 9 squares and one piece 9 by 12 squares, what more will you need to make a box? What will be the size of this box?

d) Can you make a box from two pieces of 5 by 10 squares, two pieces of 10 by 12 and two pieces of 7 by 12 squares? Why?

SOLVER SHOULD KNOW

- knowledge of nets might be helpful
- volume is not required

MATERIALS TO USE

- squared paper if boxes are actually made, scissors and Sellotape
- a box (other than a cube) to look at is helpful; being able to take it apart even more so

FOR THE TEACHER

Help the pupils make connections between the dimensions of the box and the dimensions of each face. Ask them to think about the pieces needed to make each box, and the relationship between them.

Organising Questions **2.1** (p.28)
Procedures 1.1, 1.3, 1.5, 2.1, 2.2, 2.4, 2.7, 2.13, 2.19 (pp.30–39)

Skills 1.1, **2.1, 2.2, 2.3**, 5.2, 5.3 (pp.41–44)

RESOLUTION AND NOTES

The general relationship is that a cuboid with dimensions x, y and z requires two pieces of each of the following: x by y, y by z, x by z.

a) Two pieces of 16 by 6 are required to make a box (16 by 8 by 6).
b) One piece of 6 by 8 and one piece of 4 by 6 are needed.

c) One piece of 5 by 9, one piece of 9 by 12 and two pieces of 5 by 12 are needed to make a box 5 by 9 by 12.
d) No: four dimensions are involved not three in the pieces mentioned. The 5 by 10 must be 7 by 10 or the 7 by 12 must be 5 by 12.

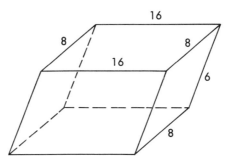

Interpretation
In parts a) and c) a non-cubical box, a parallelepiped could also be made. Cuboids are implied but it is interesting to see if the children can find this alternative.

EXTENSIONS

1 Find relationships between the parts needed to make other solids, e.g. triangular or square pyramids, triangular parallelepipeds (tent-shaped), etc.

2 What shape of paper do you need to make a cone?

18   DOUBLE DIAMOND

Start with 1, double it, double it again and so on. You will get 1, 2, 4, 8, 16, 32, 64, 128, 256 ... Look at the units digit of the numbers: *1, 2, 4, 8, 16, 32, 64, 128, 256* ... Can you see a pattern?
   This 'diamond' diagram shows the pattern:

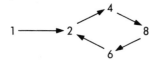

Start with 3 and keep doubling: 3, 6, 12, 24, 48, 96 ... Do you notice the pattern in the units digits? Make a diamond diagram for starting with 3. Can you see how to combine this new diamond with the diamond for starting with 1?

SOLVER SHOULD KNOW   MATERIALS TO USE

- multiplication

FOR THE TEACHER

Help pupils to focus on the root of the problem. Encourage them to look for patterns by noticing repetition and presenting the information in a visually-informative way.
   Draw their attention to any particularly helpful result, in this case the example given could be used. The problem is loosely defined so it helps to focus on the units digits and realise that the whole number does not have to be doubled.

Organising Questions **1.2, 2.2, 2.3**
  (pp.28–29)
Procedures 1.1, 1.3, 1.4, 2.1, 2.7, 2.14,
  2.17, 2.19, 3.5 (pp.30–40)

Skills 1.1, 1.2, 1.3, 1.4, **1.5**, 3.1
  (pp.41–43)

RESOLUTION AND NOTES

The basic problem is concrete but formal operational thought can be applied to it to produce systematic patterns for all multipliers.

a) *Doubling patterns*
The diagram for all doubling patterns is shown here. The only difference between starting numbers is where the main pattern is joined. Five forms its own pattern, it goes to 0 and stays there $(5 \rightarrow 10, 20, 30, 40 \dots)$.

  Numbers greater than 10 can be added to the table alongside their units digits.

b) *Multiplying-by-3 patterns*
Two diagrams are needed, one for even starting numbers and one for odd starting numbers. Again 0 and 5 are exceptions, 5 goes to 5 and stays there, 0 stays at 0.

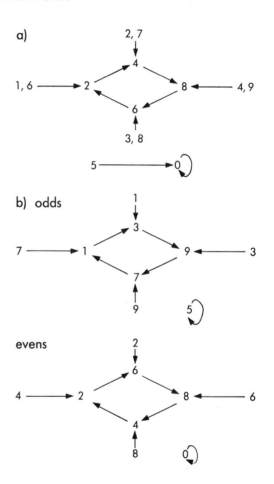

EXTENSIONS

All the 'multiplying by' patterns are interesting. This might form a small project. Some of the multiplying numbers need more than one diamond – which ones?

  The 'multiplying by' patterns for numbers depend only on their units digits, so all 'multiplying by' patterns have been done when 10 is reached.

19 LEAPFROG

On a row of five squares, two red counters and two black counters are placed like this:

R	R		B	B

The red counters can move one place to the right or they can hop over a black counter. The black counters move in the same way but to the left.

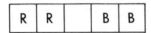

Can you finish with the black counters where the red ones were and the red counters where the black ones were? What would be the least number of moves needed?

Now try with three counters of each colour on a row of seven squares.

SOLVER SHOULD KNOW

- logical thought
- awareness of patterns other than number pattern
- ability to record actions on paper

MATERIALS TO USE

- counters (rows of squares can be drawn freehand)

FOR THE TEACHER

Encourage pupils to look for a pattern. This relates to the least number of moves and involves rules for which piece moves and in what order. Suggest trying a smaller-scale problem, say three squares and one counter of each colour.

Encourage pupils to have a system for recording the moves. To count the moves, a decision must be taken about which colour moves first.

Ask pupils to focus on the difference between jumping and sliding.

Organising Questions **2.3, 2.4** (p.29)
Procedures 1.1, 1.2, 1.4, 1.6, **1.7, 2.3,**
  2.8, 2.13, **2.17**, 2.19, 3.5 (pp.30–40)

Skills 1.3, 2.1 (pp.41–42)

RESOLUTION AND NOTES

To arrive at the solution the steps must be carried out logically. As shown in the diagram, eight moves are required to interchange the counters. Fifteen moves are required for six counters and seven squares.

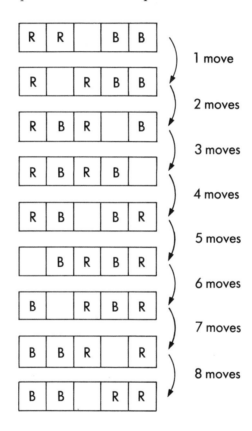

EXTENSIONS

The game can also be tried with any number of counters providing that the number of squares is at least one more than the total number of counters.

In each case, investigate whether it is possible to interchange the counters and how many moves are required. Use patterns previously discovered as much as possible.

20 SIGNPOSTS

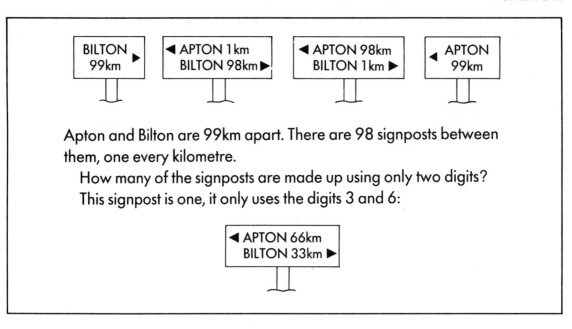

Apton and Bilton are 99km apart. There are 98 signposts between them, one every kilometre.

How many of the signposts are made up using only two digits? This signpost is one, it only uses the digits 3 and 6:

SOLVER SHOULD KNOW

- meaning of digit

MATERIALS TO USE

FOR THE TEACHER

Encourage pupils to look for a pattern. Ask them to list the ways in which two digits can be used to make the number 9.

Arranging the information systematically is important if cases are not to be missed.

━━ RESOLUTION AND NOTES ━━

The meaning of 'only two digits' may have to be made clear. The full list of signposts using only two digits is:

*	11	22	33	44	55	66	77	88	99
99	88	77	66	55	44	33	22	11	*

9	18	27	36	45	54	63	72	81	90
90	81	72	63	54	45	36	27	18	9

Children are likely to miss the second batch. If so, they can be asked to jumble up one of the first batch and see if the resulting number pair works.

Interpretation
The posts marked with an asterisk (*) are included or not, according to the interpretation given to the 'using only two digits' (the first pair use only one digit): 18 or 20 accordingly.

The same pattern will be obtained if the distance between the towns is a multiple of 11, 77, 88, 99, 110, 121 etc.

━━ EXTENSIONS ━━

1 What if Apton and Bilton were a different distance apart?

2 With what other distances would the same patterns arise?

21 FREDDY FROG

Freddy Frog is at the bottom of a well 10m deep. Each hour he climbs up 1m and then falls back 0.5m.

How long is it before Freddy is out of the well?

SOLVER SHOULD KNOW

- addition, subtraction
- some graphical approaches need skill, but can be replaced by unsophisticated ones

MATERIALS TO USE

- graph paper or squared paper may be useful
- a concrete representation of the frog might help

FOR THE TEACHER

Introduce materials to help pupils get started. Encourage representations either in pictures or using the number line, of the frog's progress.

If pupils get stuck, change the way the problem is viewed by having a smaller well.

Organising Questions **1.3, 2.6**
  (pp.28, 29)
Procedures 1.3, 1.6, 1.7, 2.7, **2.8**, 2.16,
  2.17, 2.18 (pp.31–38)

Skills 1.1, 1.3, **2.1, 2.2**, 2.3 (pp.41–42)

RESOLUTION AND NOTES

The answer is 19 hours. After 18 hours
the frog has climbed 9m. During the 19th
hour the frog climbs 1m and gets out.

Interpretation
It is possible to argue that after climbing
each metre the frog is so tired that he
slips back. When he reaches the top he is
too tired to climb out and still slips back.
He will then take about 19½ hours to get
out.

For younger children the best method is
to suggest drawing a graph. One
possibility is shown on the right. Using
this type of graph does require an
appreciation of scale and the conventions
of cartesian graphs. Less sophisticated
approaches are likely to be just as
successful especially if preceded by
trying out the graph on a smaller well,
e.g. first look at a well 3m deep.
  Different coloured pens for different
hours may reduce confusion.

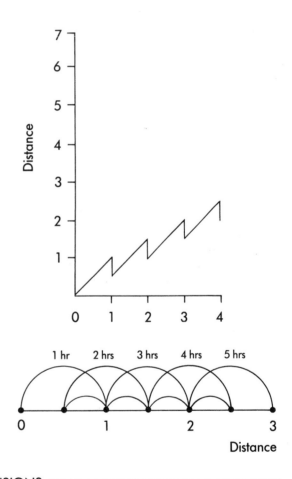

EXTENSIONS

1 Generalise to wells of different depths
(not all integral depths).

2 There are similar problems involving
two animals racing. One form is a 100m
race with one animal taking 2.3m leaps to
every 3.2m leaps by the other. Who
wins?

22 FUNNY FOURS

Can you make all the numbers from 1 to 20 using only the number 4?
You can make 8 by 4 + 4. How can you make 1?

SOLVER SHOULD KNOW

- number operations
- flexibility in approach
- knowledge of brackets useful

MATERIALS TO USE

FOR THE TEACHER

Help children make connections. For example, concentrate on the role of 1. Does that help make any number?

Apart from adding numbers, what else can be done? Making generalisations is useful, for example in making 13 from 12. Make pupils aware of possibilities by systematically recording their results.

Organising Questions **2.1, 2.6**   Skills 1.3 (p.41)
  (pp.28–29)
Procedures 1.1, 1.3, 2.0, 2.1, 2.10, **2.19,**
  3.6 (pp.30–40)

━━━━━ RESOLUTION AND NOTES ━━━━━

The operations allowed are not specified. Let the children use any they know. By adding 4s any multiple of 4 can be made: $4 + 4$ gives 8, $4 + 4 + 4$ gives 12 and so on.

    Subtracting 4s makes little difference except that 0 can be made by $4 - 4$. Since multiplication may be regarded as repeated addition, numbers made using the $\times$ sign can also be made by addition but in a more cumbersome manner. 4×4 for 16 is neater than $4 + 4 + 4 + 4$.

    Introducing division makes a difference since 1 can be written as 4/4. Using this, any number can be made. For example, 13 can be written as $4 + 4 + 4 + 4/4$.

    Some children may like to use other operations like square root. Others may want to allow $11 = 44/4$ or use 4! (read 4 factorial $= 4 \times 3 \times 2 \times 1$) or use fourth powers.

━━━━━ EXTENSIONS ━━━━━

1 3 is quite interesting but the process is very similar. Large numbers mean lots of adding on n/n and things become messy.

2 What numbers can be made using exactly four 4s?

3 A problem like this played as a game can be a good way of introducing new operations (like $\sqrt{}$) or, say, the use of brackets.

23   CROSSING THE RIVER

Two men and two boys want to cross a river. None of them can swim and they only have one canoe. They can all paddle but the canoe will only hold one man or two boys.
How do they all get across?

SOLVER SHOULD KNOW

- logical thought
- ability to record results

MATERIALS TO USE

- objects to represent boys, men and canoe (e.g. small and large rods and a box lid)

FOR THE TEACHER

Make sure the children concentrate on the information given in the problem. Focus on getting the canoe back for the second trip. Help children realise that some crossings only waste time.

Introduce materials to represent men and boys. Make sure that attempts are recorded. Children are usually very inventive in the means they use.

Organising Questions **1.1, 1.3** (p.28)
Procedures 1.1, 1.3, 1.6, **1.7**, 2.0, 2.5,
  2.13, 2.17, 2.18, 3.6 (pp.30–40)

Skills 2.1, 2.2, 2.3 (p.42)

RESOLUTION AND NOTES

This is an extremely well-known problem. To resolve it involves realising the following:

a) The canoe has to be rowed back several times.

b) It is not a good idea to use the men to row it back.

c) Whenever a man goes across there must be a boy on the far bank to row the canoe back.

d) The starting point is to send both boys across.

Resolution

		MMBB		
1	Two boys row across	MM	*	BB
2	One boy rows the canoe back	* MMB		B
3	The first man rows across	MB	*	MB
4	The second boy rows the canoe back	* MBB		M
5	As for 1	M	*	MBB
6	As for 2	* MB		MB
7	The second man rows across	B	*	MMB
8	As for 4	* BB		MM
9	As for 1		*	MMBB

The letters on the right give the positions at the end of each move. An asterisk (*) marks the position of the canoe.

EXTENSIONS

1 Find the minimum number of crossings required.

2 Vary the numbers of men and boys.

3 There are many variations on this theme. Most, such as those involving missionaries and cannibals, jealous couples or wolves, sheep and cabbages involve the extra condition that certain combinations must not be left on one bank together.

Here are six views of the same cube. Which pattern is opposite which?

Make up a cube puzzle like this.

- 3-dimensional perception

- cubes or squared paper to make them

Introduce materials to get help started.
Children could make a cube and label it.

RESOLUTION AND NOTES

The net of the cube is drawn on the right. It is easier to make a cube than to work just with the net of a cube.

It is also possible to resolve the problem without drawing at all. Either good 3-dimensional perception is required or the realisation that patterns are opposite if they are not shown as adjacent in any of the views.

The following pairs are on opposite faces: square and addition sign, circle and star, arrow and S shape.

Making up a similar cube puzzle can be instructive. Make sure that the children get the orientation of their symbols correct (e.g. distinguishing between ⟋ and ⟍).

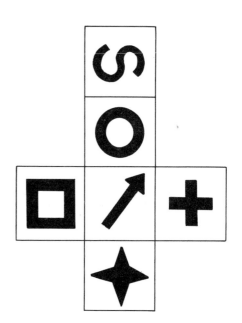

EXTENSIONS

1 How many of the six views shown are actually needed? Make up a cube puzzle which provides the smallest number of views possible.

2 It is possible to construct such problems using *any* polyhedron. How many different views are needed for a tetrahedron?

3 Make up a cube puzzle which shows some inconsistent views and pick them out.

25 SHIFTING SHAPES

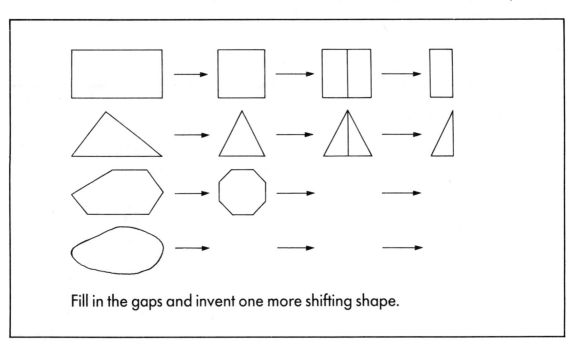

Fill in the gaps and invent one more shifting shape.

SOLVER SHOULD KNOW

- basic idea of symmetry
- some idea of regularity

MATERIALS TO USE

- pencil, paper, ruler

FOR THE TEACHER

There are many alternative solutions. Ask children to look at connections. Make sure they notice what is happening at each step, what is changing and what remains the same. Suggest they look for starting shapes which give the same end shape.

112

Organising Questions **2.1** (p.28)
Procedures 1.3, 1.4, 2.1, **2.2**, 2.7, 2.13,
   2.16, 2.19, 3.6 (pp.31–40)

Skills 1.1, 4.1, 4.2, 5.2 (pp.41–44)

RESOLUTION AND NOTES

The first step is that whatever is put in becomes as mathematically regular as possible. The relationship is many-to-one (for a one-to-one relationship see Problem 26). From the final output you cannot tell what the original input was in every detail. Any shape will assume its most regular form, for example a quadrilateral becomes a square. The last two steps are to draw a line down the middle, and take half according to the line.

Any polygon can be used to replace the question mark, or any closed curve may be inserted and will become a half circle.

If polygons with an odd number of sides are inserted they can be 'either way up' after the first stage.

EXTENSIONS

1 Try entering 3-dimensional objects: a shoe box, a rugby ball etc.

2 Problems like this are relatively easy to invent (see Problem 26).

3 The result in the final column is:

What can you say about the original shape?

4 What sort of shapes can occur in the final column?

26 FUNCTION FINDING

16 → [A] → 20 → [B] → 40 → [C] → 30 → [D] → 15

7 → [A] → 11 → [B] → 22 → [C] → 12 → [D] → 6

20 → [A] → → [B] → → [C] → → [D] →

101 → [A] → → [B] → → [C] → → [D] →

→ [A] → → [B] → 100 → [C] → → [D] →

→ [A] → → [B] → → [C] → → [D] →

Fill in the gaps of these functions.

SOLVER SHOULD KNOW

- addition, subtraction, multiplication, division
- number patterns

MATERIALS TO USE

- squared paper to help set out the solution

FOR THE TEACHER

Help the children make connections between the input number and output number at Box A, for example. Ask them to try with the other numbers given.

Suggest they discover how or why the pattern works, for example, why is the output one less than the input?

Organising Questions **2.1, 2.4**
  (pp.33–34)
Procedures 1.3, 1.4, **2.1, 2.2**, 2.7, 2.13,
  2.16, 2.19, 3.5, 3.6 (pp.30–40)

Skills 1.1, 4.1, 4.2, 5.2 (pp.41–44)

RESOLUTION AND NOTES

Box A adds 4, Box B doubles, Box C
subtracts 10 and Box D halves.
Concrete attack: Look at each box
individually and find out what they do.
Formal attack: Concentrate then on why
the output is one less than the input.

Mathematical Note
This function is:

$$x \to x + 4 \to 2(x + 4) \to 2x - 2 \to x - 1$$
$$(2x + 8)$$

EXTENSIONS

1 Children can find the relationships
between the various columns, e.g.
subtract 5 to go from B input to D output.

2

3 Such problems are easy to invent and
children usually enjoy asking friends to
solve them.

27 BUILDING BOXES

How many different rectangular boxes can be made with:
- 1 cube?
- 2 cubes?
- 3 cubes?
- 4 cubes and so on?

How can you be sure you have found them all?

SOLVER SHOULD KNOW

- older children will find a working knowledge of the divisors of a number useful
- Problem 2 might be helpful

MATERIALS TO USE

- cubes are essential for younger children

FOR THE TEACHER

Direct pupils' attention to the root of the question. Focus on the meaning of 'rectangular box' and rules for construction.

Encourage the systematic enumeration of cases.

Organising Questions **1.2, 2.5**
   (pp.30, 30)
Procedures 1.1, 1.3, 1.6, 2.0, 2.1, 2.2,
   2.3, **2.9**, 2.18, 3.5, 3.6 (pp.30–40)

Skills 1.1, 1.2, 1.3, 2.1, 2.2, 3.1
   (pp.41–43)

═══════ RESOLUTION AND NOTES ═══════

The number of rectangular boxes which can be made from n cubes depends on the divisors of n. For example with 12 cubes the boxes will be made by using combinations of the divisors of 12. These are 1, 2, 3, 4, 6, 12; the boxes therefore have dimensions (1 × 1 × 12), (1 × 2 × 6), (1 × 3 × 4), (2 × 2 × 3).

   To find all the boxes take all the pairs of divisors which multiply to make 12 and include a 1 as the third number, then look for sets of three divisors which will multiply to make 12. In this case there is only one set of three, (2 × 2 × 3). Finally don't forget (1 × 1 × 12).

Interpretation
The (1 × 1 × 12) box may not be regarded as rectangular by some children. A cube, say 2 × 2 × 2, may also cause problems.

Looking at the problem another way:

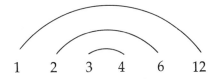

1   2   3   4   6   12

1 and 12 give (1 × 1 × 12)
2 and 6 give (1 × 2 × 6)
3 and 4 give (1 × 3 × 4).
Look at the last two and see if they can be split. 4 is 2 × 2 so we get the last box, (2 × 2 × 3)
   The divisor table from Problem 2 is useful.

═══════ EXTENSIONS ═══════

It is too hard to find a 'formula' for the number of boxes which can be made. However, investigating the types of numbers of of cubes which will make specified numbers of boxes leads to work similar to Problem 2.

28 THE FLY ON THE BOX

A fly walks along the edges of this box, starting at A and finishing at G.

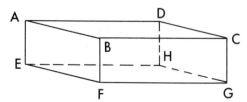

The fly never moves upwards and never walks along the same edge twice on any one journey.

How many different routes can the fly take? Sort out the routes according to the number of edges he uses. See what you can find out about the distance he walks.

SOLVER SHOULD KNOW

- logical thought
- distinction between an edge and a point
- 3-dimensional perception

MATERIALS TO USE

- a box: mark paths along edges
- different colours help distinguish different routes

FOR THE TEACHER

Help children to break down the problem. For example, fix part of route and consider the rest. Encourage children to be systematic.

Some children may think that a segment say from C to D is upwards.

Give them a box. A tree diagram may be helpful but don't suggest it too soon.

Notice that there is one point the fly can walk over more than once without breaking the rules.

STRATEGIES AND SKILLS

Organising Questions **2.5** (p.34)
Procedures and Skills 1.1, 1.3, 1.4, 1.6, 1.7, **2.0, 2.9**, 2.10, 2.13, 2.14, 2.16, 2.17, 2.18, 3.5 (pp.30–40)

Skills 1.1, 1.3, 1.5, 2.1, 2.2, 2.3, 3.1, 3.2 (pp.41–43)

There are 16 routes. In the table below they are grouped according to where the fly descends. The 'set' involved is that of thinking that because the fly must not walk along the same edge twice he may not walk through point A twice. (A is the only point that may be walked through twice without breaking the rules or finishing.)

The numbers on the right are the numbers of edges traversed. There are seven routes starting AB and seven routes starting AD. The distance walked depends on the lengths of the edges.

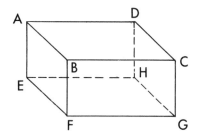

		number of edges	
down at A	AEFG	3	
	AEHG	3	
6	ADCBAEFG		7
	ADCBAEHG		7
	ABCDAEFG		7
	ABCDAEHG		7
down at B	ABFEHG		5
	ABFG	3	
4	ADCBFEHG		7
	ADCBFG		5
down at C	ADCG	3	
2	ABCG	3	
down at D	ADHG	3	
	ADHEFG		5
4	ABCDHG		5
	ABCDHEFG		7

A tree diagram is another way of showing the routes:

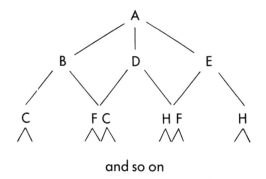

and so on

1 Change the rules: e.g. the fly can go through each point only once.

2 Change the finishing points.

3 Give dimensions to the box and then find the shortest route(s).

4 Examine different types of solid, e.g. pyramids, triangular parallelopipeds etc. or a 'multistorey box' like this:

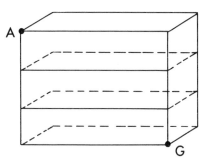

119

29 THE COLOURFUL CUBE

Use small cubes in four different colours to make a bigger cube with one of each colour on every face. Each of the small cubes must be painted in one colour only.

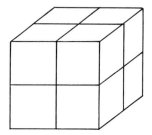

Is there only one way to do it?

SOLVER SHOULD KNOW

MATERIALS TO USE

- centicubes or other set of equal cubes in different colours
- Sellotape or other means of sticking cubes together is useful when comparing solutions

FOR THE TEACHER

Encourage children to look for patterns. Noticing where the cubes are placed may produce results. Trial and error can lead to other results.

Draw children's attention to what is meant by two solutions being 'the same'.

━━━━━━━━━━━━━ RESOLUTION AND NOTES ━━━━━━━━━━━━━

Choosing the colours red, green, yellow and blue, the larger cube is constructed as shown below:

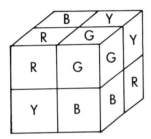

The pattern is that the two cubes of each colour are placed diagonally opposite each other one in the top layer and one in the bottom layer.

How many different (2 × 2 × 2) cubes can be made from these small cubes? Two resolutions will be different if neither one can be turned around so that the colours are in exactly the same position as on the other cube. There are just two different resolutions to the problem – the one given and its 'mirror image'. All others can be shown, by turning, to be the same as one of these.

━━━━━━━━━━━━━ EXTENSIONS ━━━━━━━━━━━━━

1 Children may be encouraged to try larger cubes and different conditions. Small cubes painted systematically in various ways can prove interesting.

2 Larger cubes, for example (3 × 3 × 3), with various constraints on the colours,

are of interest and could form the basis for a project. This is a good example of a simple problem which can be extended in all sorts of ways (P3.5, P3.6).

30   DIAGONALS

Draw four dots on a circle. Join them up.
Choose one point only and see how many
diagonals you can draw in from it.

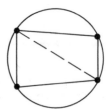

The diagram shows the results. On a new circle try the same thing
with five points. Then try six points, seven points and so on.
Make a table like this:

number of points	number of diagonals
4	1
5	2
6	3

Can you see a pattern?
If you had 100 points on a circle, how many diagonals could you
draw from one point? Explain how you know.

SOLVER SHOULD KNOW

- understanding of a diagonal
- number patterns

MATERIALS TO USE

- pencil and paper
- the circles can be drawn around a coin or freehand

FOR THE TEACHER

Encourage children to look for a pattern.
Draw their attention to the pattern of
diagonals increasing by one as well as the
relationship between the number of
points and the number of diagonals
(three less).

A new diagram is needed for each
different number of points. The points
should be well spaced round the circle.

RESOLUTION AND NOTES

The number of diagonals that can be drawn is always three less than the number of points. This is because each time there are three points to which diagonals cannot be drawn, the point chosen and the two adjacent points. The point chosen is already joined to the two adjacent points by the lines forming the sides of the polygon (which are not counted as diagonals).

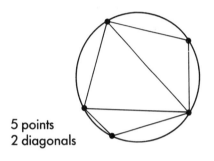

5 points
2 diagonals

The table is shown below.

number of points	number of diagonals
4	1
5	2
6	3
7	4
⋮	⋮
n	n−3

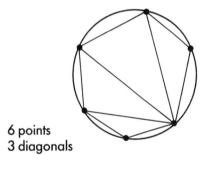

6 points
3 diagonals

EXTENSIONS

1 Look at the number patterns resulting from putting in all the diagonals. As (n−3) can be drawn from each point and there are n points, there are n(n−3) diagonals *except* that we have counted each one twice (once from each end point).

2 Total number of diagonals is therefore ½n(n−3). The number pattern resulting is very closely related to the triangular numbers (Problem 8, for example).

3 Making the diagonal diagram using curve stitching with different coloured threads can display many patterns. Try using one colour for joining points adjacent but one, another colour for adjacent but two and so on.

8 PROBLEMS 1–30

1 RABBITS AND HUTCHES

NUMERICAL

> There are some rabbits and some rabbit hutches. If seven rabbits are put in each rabbit hutch, one rabbit is left over. If nine rabbits are put in each rabbit hutch, one hutch is left empty.
>
> Can you find how many rabbit hutches and how many rabbits there are?

2 FACTORS

GENERALISATION REQUIRED, NUMERICAL

number	factors
1	1
2	1 2
3	1 • 3
4	1 2 • 4
5	1 • • • 5
6	1 2 3 • • 6

This table shows the numbers from 1 to 6 with their factors. The number 4, for example, has factors 1, 2 and 4, with no number in the space for 3.

Make your own table for the numbers up to 30. See what you can find out about numbers with only two factors. Can you guess the next one? What sort of numbers are they?

Now try three factors and then four factors. See if you can guess the next number with three factors and then with four, and explain why. What sort of numbers have an odd number of factors? Can you find other patterns in your table?

3   THE MILK CRATE

A milk crate holds 24 bottles and is shaped like this:

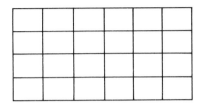

The crate has four rows and six columns. Can you put 18 bottles of milk in the crate so that each row and each column of the crate has an *even* number of bottles in it? Is there only one way to do it?

4   CROSSING THE DESERT

A man has to deliver a message across a desert. Crossing the desert takes nine days. One man can only carry enough food to last him 12 days. No food is available where the message must be delivered. Two men set out.

   Can the message be delivered and both men return to where they started without going short of food? (Food may be buried on the way out and used on the way back.)

5 MAKING TOAST

There is room in a grill to toast one side of two slices of bread in two minutes. How long does it take to toast both sides of three slices of bread? Is that the quickest way?

Work out the quickest way to toast four slices of bread on both sides. Then try five slices of bread and then six. Can you predict the quickest time for any number of slices? How would you do it? Try again with a grill that holds three or more slices of bread.

6 MAKING TRIANGLES

Using 12 rods of varying lengths how many different triangles can you make?

What *types* of triangle can you make? Can you make a triangle with *any* three rods? What about 2, 3 and 5 or 2, 2 and 3?

7   NO TRIANGLES ALLOWED

Draw four dots on a circle and join each dot to the
next dot with a straight line. Can you draw any
more straight lines, joining up the dots *without*
making any triangles?

   Try the same thing for five dots, six dots, seven
dots and so on, getting in as many lines as you can.
Can you fill in a table of the number of dots and
number of lines? Predict how many lines can be
drawn without making triangles when there are 13
dots. What sort of number never appears in the
second column of the table?

8   VILLAGE STREETS

In a village there are three streets. All the streets are straight. One
lamp-post is put up at each crossroads.

   What is the greatest number of lamp-posts that could be needed?
Now try four streets and five streets. Predict the answer for six streets
then check it. Can you see a pattern? Why does the pattern work?

9   AFTERNOON TEA PARTY

Some people had afternoon tea in a cafe which only sold tea and cakes. Tea cost 3p a cup, cakes cost 5p each. Everyone had the same number of cakes and the same number of cups of tea. The bill came to £1.33.

Can you find out how many cups of tea each person had?

10   PERFECT NUMBERS

What numbers go into 6 exactly? 6, 3, 2 and 1 do. Do you notice that $6 = 3 + 2 + 1$? 6 is called a *perfect* number because it is equal to the sum of the other numbers which go into it exactly.

What is the next perfect number?

11   CHANGING FIFTY PENCE

The other day I was asked if I could change a 50 pence piece. I had more than 50 pence in coins in my pocket but I could not make exactly 50 pence.

Can you find several ways this could happen? What is the largest amount I could have had in my pocket?

12 BADMINTON GAME

Janet, Sangita, Anne and Margaret like to play badminton together but cannot all be free to play on the same day. Janet is unable to play on Tuesdays, Wednesdays and Saturdays. Sangita is free to play on Mondays, Wednesdays and Thursdays. Anne has to stay at home on Mondays and Thursdays. Margaret can play on Mondays, Tuesdays and Fridays. None of them play on Sundays.

Can each pair find a day on which to play? Are there any days when no games can be played? Are there any days when more than one game can be played?

13 TWO TOWERS

A child has a set of 10 cubes. One cube has 1 cm edges, one cube has 2 cm edges, one cube has 3 cm edges and so on until the largest cube which has 10 cm edges.

Can she build two towers of the same height using all the cubes? Show how, or explain why, it can't be done. What difference does it make if another cube with 11 cm edges is used as well? Show how to do it in as many ways as possible.

14   A RECTANGLE

The perimeter of a rectangle is 28cm. The length is 10cm more than the width.

What is its length? What is its area? What if the difference were 8cm?

15   PACKING BOXES

Place some boxes with bases 8cm by 6cm on a tray 50cm by 35cm.

If all the boxes have to be placed the same way round, what is the greatest number of boxes which can be placed on the tray? Does it make any difference if the boxes don't all have to be placed on it the same way? What is the greatest number of boxes which can be placed on the tray?

16   PUT THE LID ON

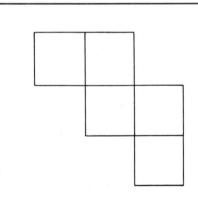

Make a large copy of this shape. Cut it out and fold it up; it will make a box.

Where could you add another square onto the shape so that when you cut it out and fold it up you will get a box with a lid?

Find as many shapes as you can which will fold into a box with a lid.

17   MARY'S MUDDLE

Mary had two pieces of squared paper, 16 by 8 squares and two pieces 8 by 6 squares.

a) How many more pieces does she need to make a box? What size will the pieces be? What size will the box be?

b) Now begin with two pieces of squared paper 4 by 8 squares, one piece of paper 6 by 8 squares and one piece 4 by 6 squares. What else will you need to make a box?

c) If you have one piece of paper 5 by 9 squares and one piece 9 by 12 squares, what more will you need to make a box? What will be the size of this box?

d) Can you make a box from two pieces of 5 by 10 squares, two pieces of 10 by 12 and two pieces of 7 by 12 squares? Why?

18   DOUBLE DIAMOND

Start with 1, double it, double it again and so on. You will get 1, 2, 4, 8, 16, 32, 64, 128, 256 ... Look at the units digit of the numbers: *1, 2, 4, 8, 16, 32, 64, 128, 256* ... Can you see a pattern?

This 'diamond' diagram shows the pattern:

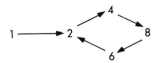

Start with 3 and keep doubling: 3, 6, 12, 24, 48, 96 ... Do you notice the pattern in the units digits? Make a diamond diagram for starting with 3. Can you see how to combine this new diamond with the diamond for starting with 1?

On a row of five squares, two red counters and two black counters are placed like this:

R	R		B	B

The red counters can move one place to the right or they can hop over a black counter. The black counters move in the same way but to the left.

Can you finish with the black counters where the red ones were and the red counters where the black ones were? What would be the least number of moves needed?

Now try with three counters of each colour on a row of seven squares.

20 SIGNPOSTS

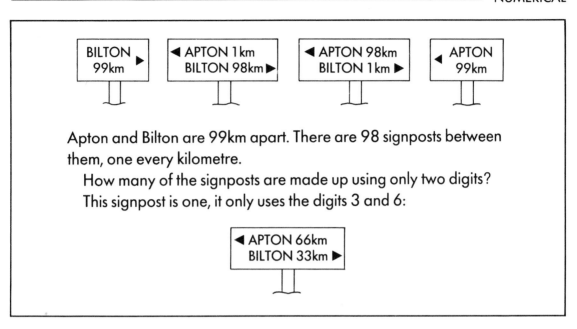

Apton and Bilton are 99km apart. There are 98 signposts between them, one every kilometre.

How many of the signposts are made up using only two digits? This signpost is one, it only uses the digits 3 and 6:

21 FREDDY FROG

Freddy Frog is at the bottom of a well 10m deep. Each hour he climbs up 1m and then falls back 0.5m.

How long is it before Freddy is out of the well?

22 FUNNY FOURS

Can you make all the numbers from 1 to 20 using only the number 4? You can make 8 by 4 + 4. How can you make 1?

23   CROSSING THE RIVER

Two men and two boys want to cross a river. None of them can swim and they only have one canoe. They can all paddle but the canoe will only hold one man or two boys.
How do they all get across?

24   CUBE PUZZLE

Here are six views of the same cube. Which pattern is opposite which?

Make up a cube puzzle like this.

25 SHIFTING SHAPES

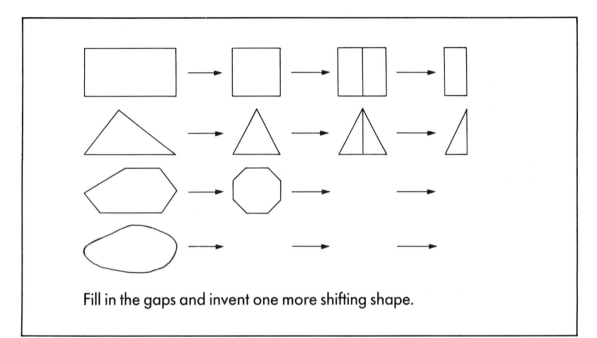

Fill in the gaps and invent one more shifting shape.

26 FUNCTION FINDING

16 ⟶ A ⟶ 20 ⟶ B ⟶ 40 ⟶ C ⟶ 30 ⟶ D ⟶ 15

7 ⟶ A ⟶ 11 ⟶ B ⟶ 22 ⟶ C ⟶ 12 ⟶ D ⟶ 6

20 ⟶ A ⟶ ⟶ B ⟶ ⟶ C ⟶ ⟶ D ⟶

101 ⟶ A ⟶ ⟶ B ⟶ ⟶ C ⟶ ⟶ D ⟶

⟶ A ⟶ ⟶ B ⟶ 100 ⟶ C ⟶ ⟶ D ⟶

⟶ A ⟶ ⟶ B ⟶ ⟶ C ⟶ ⟶ D ⟶

Fill in the gaps of these functions.

27   BUILDING BOXES

GENERALISATION REQUIRED, NUMERICAL, SPATIAL, COMBINATORICS

How many different rectangular boxes can be made with:
  1 cube?
  2 cubes?
  3 cubes?
  4 cubes and so on?
How can you be sure you have found them all?

28   THE FLY ON THE BOX

SPATIAL, LOGICAL

A fly walks along the edges of this box, starting at A and finishing at G.

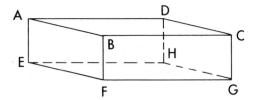

The fly never moves upwards and never walks along the same edge twice on any one journey.

   How many different routes can the fly take? Sort out the routes according to the number of edges he uses. See what you can find out about the distance he walks.

SPATIAL

Use small cubes in four different colours to make a bigger cube with one of each colour on every face. Each of the small cubes must be painted in one colour only.

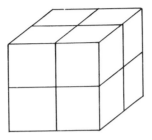

Is there only one way to do it?

30 DIAGONALS

GENERALISATION REQUIRED, NUMERICAL, SPATIAL

Draw four dots on a circle. Join them up.
Choose one point only and see how many diagonals you can draw in from it.

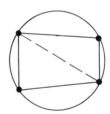

The diagram shows the results. On a new circle try the same thing with five points. Then try six points, seven points and so on.
Make a table like this:

number of points	number of diagonals
4	1
5	2
6	3

Can you see a pattern?
If you had 100 points on a circle, how many diagonals could you draw from one point? Explain how you know.

BIBLIOGRAPHY

Armstrong, M., *Closely Observed Children*, Writers and Readers Publishing Co-operative Society Ltd., 1980

Balacheff, N., *Une Approche Experimentale pour l'étude des processus de resolution de problèmes*, Proceedings of the 5th Conference of the International Group for the Psychology of Mathematics Education, Grenoble, 1981

Banwell, C., Saunders, K. and Tahta, D., *Starting Points*, Oxford University Press, 1972

Brown, S. and Walker, M., *The Art of Problem Posing*, Franklin Institute Press, 1983

Burton, L., 'Problems and Puzzles' in *For the Learning of Mathematics*, vol. 1, no. 2, 1980

Burton, L., 'What can you find out about odd and even numbers?' in *Mathematics Teaching*, no. 97, 1981

Cockcroft, Dr W.H. (Chairman), *Mathematics Counts: report of the Committee of Inquiry into the Teaching of Mathematics in Schools*, H.M.S.O., 1982

Cundy, M.H. and Rollett, A.P., *Mathematical Models*, Oxford University Press, 1961

Guillerant, M. and Co., *Une Experience de lecture en géometrie*, 3rd Colloquium on Language Aquisition, Ghent, Belgium, 1983

Harlen, W., Darwin, A. and Murphy, M., *Match and Mismatch: Finding Answers*, Oliver and Boyd, for the Schools Council, 1977

Mason, J., Burton, L. and Stacey, K., *Thinking Mathematically*, Addison-Wesley Publishers Ltd., 1982

Mottershead, L., *Sources of Mathematical Discovery*, Basil Blackwell, 1979